Fearless Ghost

The Return

by

Alex Scott

Published by
You Suddenly Smiled Books
1 Broomdene Avenue
Castle Bromwich
Birmingham B34 6PJ

FOREWORD
by Dr. Carl Chinn

Think of railway towns and where comes to mind? Swindon and Crewe jump forward immediately, and as for a city connected strongly with railways, then what better candidate could there be than York? Few people would suggest Birmingham as a place tied into railways and yet the City of a Thousand Trades can also proclaim a deep bond with locomotives.

Railways affected deeply the look and shape of Birmingham. They also had a profound impact upon its economic life. Railway companies employed thousands of folk in Brum - and not only with regard to passenger trains, for the city was a major entrepot for the movement of goods. There were great goods yards in Lawley Street, Hockley and elsewhere, and as a result a number of districts became noted for the residence of large numbers of railwaymen and their families - Alum Rock, Saltley, parts of Nechells, Vauxhall, Acocks Green and Tyseley among them.

It is not surprising that the presence of so many steam trains in Birmingham acted as a strong and attractive magnet to young lads. One of those lads was Alex Scott. He was born within the sound of Aston loco sheds, code 21D, which was both the main passenger depot for New Street station and a freight depot. With that wonderland so close to him, it is little wonder that Alex became one of tens of thousands of Brummie kids who became passionate train spotters. But, unlike many, Alex took his passion further. He didn't just wait for the trains to come to him, he and his pals went out looking for them - any kind no matter how humble. In this way he became skilled at 'bunking' - sneaking into engine sheds and workshops so as to cop the numbers of engines.

The story of Alex's bunking is told evocatively in Fearless Ghosts. Here in Fearless Ghost - The Return, Alex takes up his tale from today's perspective. He goes back to all the sheds he bunked as a youngster. Some are still standing, others are gone. But with a keen eye and a perceptive awareness of that which has disappeared, Alex brings back to life a world to which he belonged. That world has all but been swept away, but because of Alex Scott's ability and empathy it will not be forgotten.

ISBN 0-9540834-0-7
Copyright © Alex Scott 2001
All rights reserved . This book is sold on the condition that no part of it may be reproduced in any form whatsoever be re-sold hired out or otherwise circulated by any means including electronic means and broadcasting without the publisher's prior written consent.

Printed by Crystal Print Services, Birmingham, 0121 - 773 9094

Contents

Page 4   Homeward Bound
Page 11 1998 - the trip of a lifetime
Page 12 In the beginning
Page 14 The tin loco
Page 21 Revisiting old haunts
Page 34 List of sheds visited 1960-66
Page 35 "Look everyone, Alex has come to visit us!"
Page 39 What's here today, Saturday 17th July, 1999
Page 44 Vandals and Cannibals
Page 45 Uncanny to arrive here today
Page 50 Worcester, the aftermath
Page 52 A different type of eclipse
Page 60 Today we're in cider country
Page 66 Almost to the day
Page 68 Thoughts of Nan and Grandad
Page 76 The Fleetwood Macs
Page 78 This could be the last time!
Page 82 A wet and wonderful day in South Wales.
Page 88 With tears in my eyes
Page 92 "Sorry lad, you're a week too late."
Page 97 Down the dip into Sheffield Midland
Page 103 A bevy of beauties in Bristol and Bath
Page 107 Another magical day!
Page 110 The longest haul
Page 125 The warmth of an April morning
Page 129 We weren't exactly singing in the rain
Page 135 The end of the line
Page 150 I wasn't entirely satisfied
Page 155 I never covered all eighteen but I did cover thirteen
Page 160 The chicken run

Fame at last! Opening the International Balti Brasserie in August, 2000.

3

HOMEWARD BOUND

On Tuesday, 19th September, 2001, I'll be 53 years of age. Since my birth at 11.45pm on a chilly September night in 1948, I can honestly say that my days, weeks, months and years have been filled with one adventure after another.

I arrived to cheers so loud that only the cheers from the madding crowd in Ben Hur could ever have surpassed them. The world must have cheered at my arrival; how else could anyone explain the lifetime of adventures which followed?

Some of those adventures are recounted in my first book, Fearless Ghosts, which ends with the sentence "just after the 1969 holiday season, I left Weymouth for Germany but that's another story." This then is the eagerly-awaited sequel.

I was sitting in a small but cosy cafe on the dockside in Harwich. I'd ordered sausage, eggs, chips and beans, plus bread and butter and a large mug of tea. The cafe was chock-a-block with truckers and passengers waiting for incoming or departing ferries, and Joe Public in general. I was "orf" to Hamburg, Germany, so a bellyfull of hot grub was certainly warranted.

I'd sat there patiently for ten minutes or so, yet still no sign of any scoff heading my way so I decided to head in the direction from which my scoff was due to come - namely the kitchen. On arrival at my destination, I was confronted by the sight of this chap flying around the kitchen in a vain attempt to get all his customers' orders out on to their tables and eventually eaten. However, because he had only one flustered young girl trying her best to help out, I could see he was in the sh...er...proverbial.

"Need any help, mate?," I asked.

He spun round and said: "Take those orders out for me, would ya please?", nodding in the direction of a long table where all the meals stood. "All the orders are numbered, so just take them through and shout out the order number," he added.

I grabbed two plates, glanced at the numbers placed by each meal and backed through the swing door with them.

On turning to face the customers, I met with a scene resembling something out of a Carry On film. Unable to spot Barbara Windsor, I walked forward into the melee calling out: "Order number six and order number nine!"

"Number six over here!," a chap shouted.

I dropped his order off just as a young lad called out: "Mine's number nine - with extra chips!"

I spent the next half hour running round carrying everything but the kitchen sink.

  Suddenly and strangely all the once disgruntled diners were eating their meals in a contented and relaxed atmosphere. I must have lost a stone and a half running around this establishment. My own meal was soon forthcoming and I tucked into it with all the finesse of a hungry wolf. I must admit it tasted scrumptious.

  Once everyone had eaten and I'd finished my meal, I returned to "work" and collected the dirty dishes and cutlery, and helped with the mountains of washing-up. When all utensils had been returned to their rightful receptacles, I bade the gaffer farewell. To my complete and utter surprise, he offered me a full time job and digs. I thought for a moment, but my destiny was across the water. I shook his hand and regretfully turned down the job. I didn't offer to pay for my meal and I don't recall him asking.

  The ferry from Harwich to Hamburg was a real nightmare. The crossing took just over 21 hours and to say I wasn't feeling too good would be an understatement. All the passengers seemed to be either coming from or going to the toilet. I actually thought at one point that the vessel was going to keel over.

  We eventually docked and my first act was to literally sprint down the stairway on to solid ground - where my legs buckled and I fell over. A passer-by said something in German, then helped me to my feet. "Thank....thankyou," I stammered.

  I few moments later I was being ushered towards the customs area by a very official looking chap. Once through customs I purchased a railway ticket to Minden. My adventures in a foreign country were about to begin.

  I successfully negotiated the first part of my journey, arriving in Hanover where I was to change trains for Minden. It was early in the morning and I stood on a very cold platform with only my thoughts for company. Suddenly, a railway official approached but, as he spoke in German, I hadn't a clue what he was saying. The obvious thing to do was to show him my ticket and passport, which I did. He studied them closely. His next comment made me smile; it was like something out of those war comics - "Ah, Englander!" Then he continued speaking in German and directed me towards a timetable. He continued to speak, despite my obvious ignorance of his language, while pointing out the next service to Minden.

  I glanced at an overhanging clock with a second hand that ticked away lazily. "An hour before my train to Minden is due to arrive," I said to myself. Then he beckoned me towards his small office. "What's up now?," I thought. I followed in some consternation but my fears were soon laid to rest. Inside, he proffered me a hot mug of coffee and a choice of several tasty looking sandwiches - no doubt part of his lunch.

We sat together eating for almost half an hour. He said nothing, merely glancing at me once or twice. A coal fire burnt brightly in the hearth a few yards from where we were sitting. A second mug of coffee was silently produced and we just sat there slowly sipping our drinks.

The silence was broken by the shrill of an approaching locomotive. I looked at my watch and was surprised to see that an hour had passed so quickly. We stood up together and shook each other's hand, after which he ushered me out of his office and onto the train now sitting in the station. It departed on time, of course. I stood with my head hanging out of the carriage window, waving to him as the train pulled away, until he was eventually out of sight.

The compartment was very warm and my eyes were just closing when the ticket collector entered. He spoke several words in German but, of course, I had no idea what he was saying. I handed him my ticket which he clipped while twice mentioning the word "Bielefeld." I wondered what this might mean and the only sensible thing I came up with was that I had to change again, this time at Bielefeld.

After what seemed like hours of travelling, I arrived there. The time on the station clock was 3.58am. By now I was totally shattered - but another twist lay in wait. The train left and I stood alone on another quiet platform at another ghostly station. Time passed and then I heard the sound of footsteps approaching, getting closer and closer.

Once again, a railway official was advancing on me and speaking to me in German. Again, not understanding what was required of me, I produced my travel ticket and passport. These were studied with even greater intensity this time, apparently causing the official some concern as his politely helpful attitude seemed to change to a moody suspiciousness.

He was still studying my ticket and passport with sullen concentration as he led me towards his office. Thoughts of deja vu entered my head as my body was marched into a private room within a rather large looking building. An even more official-looking official was in the room, apparently eating his lunch. The two officials conversed while the second studied my ticket and passport with the same serious concentration. After a while he glanced in my direction. I watched as he lifted his heavy frame out of his comfortable looking armchair. In his hand were my ticket and passport. He looked at me several times and at the passport several times. He was obviously trying to decide if I and the person in the passport photograph were one and the same.

Then, to my surprise, he asked in English: "Where have you come from?" I was about to answer when he followed up with: "Are you army - military -

soldier?"

"Tourist," I answered.

"Tourist? Not soldier or military?," he enquired.

"No, tourist," I replied again.

He returned to his seat and picked up a telephone. He spoke for several minutes but to whom I had no idea. I heard several trains pass through the station as I sat there in patient anticipation of - what?

My eyes began to close with tiredness; however, the worry of not knowing what my position was kept me partially awake. A large, chipped mug containing coffee was handed to me, plus a handful of mixed, broken biscuits. I sat there awaiting my fate as the clock on my left ticked quietly away.

I had just washed the last piece of broken biscuit down with the last mouthful of coffee when I heard a knock at the door and in walked two military policemen. The two railway officials handed them my passport and ticket and, ominously, left me on my own with these two gun-toting gentlemen.

"Right son, you seem to be a little lost," the taller of the two stated.

At that point, I answered, "Yes, sir."

"According to your ticket your destination is Minden, so how come you're in Bielefeld?"

I explained my circumstances to him how a railway official at Hanover had very kindly placed me on a train to Minden, but that on arriving at Bielefeld I had gained the impression that I had to change trains again.

Both MPs looked at me closely and then looked at each other. The MP who hadn't spoken picked up the phone and dialled several numbers. I assumed he was phoning Hanover station to speak to my railway official friend. After some minutes he replaced the phone and said something very quietly to his partner.

"Do you know what is significant about this particular station and the surrounding area?"

"No sir, I have no idea," was my honest answer.

A short pause followed and then the taller of the two continued: "Bielefeld is a massive British military installation, and that's why we're here."

"Ah," I said. "I'm beginning to understand the concern over my unannounced arrival - but I am a British citizen."

"That remains to be seen," he said severely, before relaxing into a smile.

I was led away to an awaiting military vehicle, passing the two German railway officials en-route. The time was 4.45am.

Inside the vehicle I tried to see where we were going but the darkness of that morning made it difficult. I had no idea how far we had travelled but we stopped suddenly outside a darkened building. One of the MPs entered it, returning within seconds.

"Alex, you come with us, son," said the MP, gesturing me to follow. The other MP and I joined him and we entered the building together. I was in for another surprise.

An elderly gentleman stood just inside the entrance and directed us towards a table and three chairs. The two MPs and I sat down together. After a while, the elderly chap returned with three large meals and three large glasses full to the brim with beer.

"Tuck in, lad!," the MPs said simultaneously.

For the first time since my departure from Harwich I felt at ease. We sat together, eating and talking, until the taller MP said that their shift was over at 06.00 hours and that my train to Minden went at 06.20. We parted company on Bielefeld station at twenty to six when they both shook hands with me and wished me a safe and enjoyable holiday in Germany. At that point they left without looking back, although I waved until their vehicle disappeared from view. I must admit to a feeling of sadness at their departure, as they had shown such genuine concern for a young fellow countryman's well-being while in a foreign land.

The train to Minden duly arrived. I boarded it with a feeling of anticipation in my heart, but the time passed quickly and some hours later I was alighting in Minden to be greeted by the delightful warmth of a summer's day. The station was extremely busy, making the task of finding the connection to Loccum, my final destination, very difficult. Fortunately, a friendly, English-speaking young girl took pity on me and told me that I would have to travel to Leese, the nearest station to the small village of Loccum. She even bought my ticket for me and put me on the right train. In all the excitement I even forgot to pay her for my ticket.

Leese wasn't too far but, on arrival, I still had to find where Loccum was. After a number of confused and confusing encounters I was eventually led, almost by the hand, in the direction of Loccum. I have no idea how far I had walked when, as luck would have it, a passing motorist stopped to ask me the nearest way to some local town. I explained that I was English and that I was trying to get to a small place called Loccum. I registered his look of astonishment but, recovering, he fiddled with a map lying on the unoccupied passenger seat. I heard him mumbling away in his native tongue until, suddenly, with a smile on his face, "Loccum, Loccum," he repeated and invited me to climb in. A lift to Loccum had been uppermost in my mind for some time, so I jumped in with alacrity. We drove through the countryside, passing signs to village after unknown village until, after about half an hour and without warning, we drove into the small village of Loccum.

We bade each other farewell and off he drove, leaving me on the grassy verge at the edge of the village. I immediately sat down. The warmth of that sunny morning made me sleepy, but I lit a cigarette and gently puffed away with a feeling of contentment in my heart. Finishing my fag, and being very tired, I allowed myself to drift "orf" to sleep. I was awakened by someone prodding my ribs with what felt like a very solid object.

Stirring uncomfortably out of a deep sleep, I became aware that the object was a large walking stick held by an elderly gentleman. All the time he was poking me in the ribs he was also speaking to me - in unintelligible German, of course. I didn't know what to think apart from: "I wish you would stop poking me in the ribs with that bloody stick!"

I got to my feet and said: "Good morning! Good morning!"

At this, he looked at me, took off his cap, scratched his head and then ambled away.

I rubbed my eyes, picked up my rucksack and headed in the direction of the village square. The entire village was as picturesque as anyone could imagine. It appeared as if suspended in a motionless time-warp - a time that had been long forgotten. I was brought back to the present by the ringing of a cyclist's bell, and the spell was broken.

I stayed in this charming village for three months - and what took place in those three very enjoyable months? A clue? My first three days were spent in a convent and all my meals were served to me by nuns. I was having plenty but they were having nun of it.

In a very short time I befriended the local chemists, Herr Eberheart and Frau Arrends and lived with them at their shop for the rest of my stay.

I spent my time in Loccum learning to drive, learning the language, enjoying myself, shopping, going to various towns and cities, visiting their friends all over Germany. I had to leave when a close family friend came to stay and they needed the room. They did pay my fare home, though. I visited them again several months later but only stayed for one week.

I lived in this building for three months, staying with Herr Eberheart and Frau Arrends, the local chemists.

During my stay in Loccum, I also became friends with a young lady, Christina Meek. This is her and me outside a local farm yard in Alte Postrasse.

1998 - THE TRIP OF A LIFETIME

Do you remember the railway lines of yesteryear which took millions of people on a variety of journeys? How many of you were, like me, spending so many pleasurable hours travelling around this great country of ours for just one reason? Train spotting!

We all have our own personal and private reasons why we travelled to those destinations - to visit friends or to go on that dream summer holiday that your folks had planned; or perhaps you travelled to work by train. For me, the excitement of travelling by train was the happiest experience of my life: those unforgettable train spotting moments - magical, mysterious, marvellous, mad and at times even dangerous.

The countless hours we spent on stations, the long yards and carriage sidings passed en-route; the smell of steam coming out of the chimneys of those wonderful locomotives - all are now just fond memories held in my heart. Were you, I repeat, ever one of us - a train spotter? How many loco sheds did you "bunk" or visit without a pass or permit? Then again, were you, like me, in your day, hurrying and scurrying head first into every shed with just one thing on your mind: "I must get all the locos on shed before anyone else sees me or a size ten boot finds my backside!"

I was in and out so fast no-one even knew I'd ever visited those famous workshops with their patient parties waiting to get in. Crewe, Derby, Doncaster, Eastleigh, Swindon and Glasgow Cowlairs and St. Rollox - irresistible magnets to a fanatic like me. I bunked them all without pass or permit.

We were all so young in those great days of steam. My only interest was in the collecting and writing down of every loco: the holiday trains packed to capacity which took endless people to far-off places - holiday camps, b & bs, hotels, camp sites and chalets; trains which carried munitions, coal and minerals to keep our great country going during those hard post-war times; and troup trains, carrying our boys to and from their postings, everyone on board just wanting to get home to their loved ones - all grist to the dedicated spotter's mill.

We, the travellers and the spotters, owe an unpayable debt of gratitude to those depot foremen, clerks, locomotive drivers, firemen, signalmen and guards, and to all railway staff nationwide - all the men and women who gave their time, energy and life to the railways. And let's give a special mention to those mums and dads who lit the fires of life so that we could enjoy those untroubled days of youth - thanks!

IN THE BEGINNING

In the beginning I wrote all the locomotive numbers down on scrap paper, but I soon progressed to writing them in my old school arithmetic book. Finally, in the early Sixties, I bought some pads from Boot's in the centre of Birmingham. However, in the process of moving house to Weymouth in 1966, some of those priceless pads got lost.

These pads contained all the engine numbers from my early train spotting trips, made in the company of my two school chums, Melvin Davies and David Burrows. For example, on my first visit to London we bunked several sheds on a beautiful summer's morning, one Sunday in early June, 1961. We visited other areas during those wonderful summer months, including depots in Liverpool, Leeds and Manchester - not places of romance to most people, but in the dying days of steam unforgettable to us.

I still have the four remaining pads forty years on containing the numbers of every locomotive I spotted when visiting as many of the depots on the old British Railways system as time, finance and the spirit of adventure made possible. On the opening stage of the earliest remaining pad is recorded the fact that I visited Birmingham New Street station on 11th June, 1962 - a quiet Sunday morning, I remember. I noted 16 steam locomotives and six diesels. I "copped" - spotted for the first time - just two.

At New Street I boarded the local service to Derby but alighted at Saltley station where I whizzed round the shed. I dodged myself in and out of the three enclosed roundhouses, of which No.2 shed was the biggest, containing the majority of the 119 mixed locomotives that were regularly housed there. In all that day I copped a grand total of five engines. The lack of cops shows that I visited the depot on a regular basis.

On Monday, 12th June, 1962, I spent my time after school sitting on a small bench collecting numbers at Perry Barr station. I observed 47 mixed locomotives - steam, diesel etc. - that hauled both passenger and freight. Some travelled in a northerly direction towards Bescot and beyond, while others travelled south and east to Aston, Coventry and beyond.

In fact, a great variety of local service engines - all steam-powered - headed in every direction possible on the complicated rail network, a massive sea of railway lines linking New Street, Lichfield, Walsall or Wolverhampton. These local trains stopped at every small station en-route, out and return, day in, day out, without fail. Today there's no evidence that some stations, many signal boxes and sidings galore ever existed.

On Tuesday 13th June, 1962, I spent the evening at New Street, Aston and Saltley respectively, where I observed 70 locomotives but copped only one. The next day, Melvin and I bunked 21D Aston, where we noted 50 locos either in the shed or passing on freight and passenger workings. I did not cop a single engine that Wednesday.

We made regular trips to Aston, Saltley, New Street, Snow Hill and Tamworth throughout that June.

On Sunday, 1st July, 1962, we made a trip to London which, despite for some reason missing out shed 1A, Willesden, was triumphant. The total number of mixed locomotives we observed en-route and at the three depots we bunked - 81A Old Oak Common, 34A King's Cross and 70A Nine Elms - was 316, and I copped 93 that day.

Black Five class 4-6-0 No. 45038 at 21D Aston shed on 14th June, 1962. *(Alex Scott)*

THE TIN LOCO

The first toy locomotive I ever saw was an old wind-up loco that I held in my left hand at a large shopping store, Henry's. The store was situated towards the top end of Union Street, Birmingham, and it was Christmas, 1955. My mom paid just three old pennies for the photograph to be taken and developed. Father Christmas gave me a small gift, a little colouring book, but I wanted the loco.

My second encouter with engines, apart from seeing steam-hauled trains on holiday, was at Aston station. I stood on the old wooden platform late one afternoon in 1956. A small black locomotive approached close to where I was standing. It frightened me as it approached. The loco stopped directly opposite me and seemed to be looking menacingly at me. I just stared at it but I couldn't move.

Suddenly, a shrill from its whistle made me jump, then it moved off. I followed it momentarily out of sight but what then came into view was something else. In the distance I could see some other locomotives. They appeared to be on fire as I could see smoke, both black and white, engulf-

Black Five 4-6-0 No. 45104 passes the old wooden platform at Aston station with empty coaching stock on 19th June, 1963. (*Alex Scott*)

ing them as it rose skywards.

Strangely, I felt a pulling of my person. A strange force was pulling me down the double flight of stairs. I was then being hauled across the main Lichfield Road, then under the railway bridge and up Holborn Hill. It was at this point that the force that was dragging me stopped and left me facing a very high brick wall. The wall was too high for me to climb, but two passers-by gave me a bunk-up.

I sat on the wall just dangling my legs over the side. What I saw had to be seen to be believed. I was looking at a variety of steam locomotives. They were outside a large looking building. I could see other locos sticking

Locomotives on Aston shed, 21D, and passing by, 14th June, 1962

Steam

Fairburn Class 4 2-6-4T: 42168/267
Stanier Class 4 2-6-4T: 42488/577
Hughes Fowler Class 5 2-6-0: 42874/934
Stanier Class 5 2-6-0: 42974/9
4F 0-6-0: 44110/301/114/92/514/7
Class 5 4-6-0: 44758/862/5/72/5038/65/317/95/446
Patriot 4-6-0: 45545
Jubilee 4-6-0: 45593/617/47/740
Ivatt Class 2 2-6-0: 46423/56/70/92
3F 0-6-0T: 47341/494
8F 2-8-0: 48335/460/548/719/52
Britannia 4-6-2: 70024/9/47

Diesel

English Electric Type 4: D255/337/40/1
Sulzer Type 2: D5012

Total   Steam: 42 Diesel: 5

15

their noses out of the building. They reminded me of horses looking out of their stable doors. In the years that followed I came to know this building as Aston sheds. It was a 12-road straight shed, coded 21D.........my love affair had begun.

Sadly, the shed closed in 1965. Since its closure one or two firms have used the site for their own private businesses. To this day in the 21st century, Flight's coaches occupy a new office block on the old shed area.

The other Birmingham sheds have long gone but, as at Aston, some of the old brickwork still stands as a reminder of that great era. An era that attracted both young and old to this most fascinating of hobbies.

I have so many happy memories of all the trips that were once part of my life. I visited and bunked so many steam sheds, yards, carriage sidings and workshops over the years between 1960 and 1968 - and never had a pass or permit for any of them. I only ever saw one and that was outside Crewe Works many years ago. In actual fact, it was Sunday, 15th July, 1962. I was a young lad then, nearly 14.

The memories I have from those days are still closely linked by my love of those happy times. The locos are just a thing of the past, but the love I hold dear to my heart will not leave me, even though I'm 51.

The hobby of train spotting was a very simple one but, oh so dangerous. I've brushed against the shoulders of death on more than one occasion, beyond that cat's nine lives.

The most significant change is in the reduction of locomotives one can now observe. The depots that housed them, from a couple of little tank locos to those which, on a good day, contained anything up to a hundred plus, are gone. All that remains today are private railways, photos, books, and magazines.

I think train spotting was like any hobby - fishing, bird watching, football, cricket but it was a nationwide hobby. I personally covered tens of thousands of miles for the love of this hobby.

The first shed I ever visited and bunked was a Great Western shed - Tyseley. The code was 84E. I bunked it with Melvin and David, my two chums from Birchfield Road secondary modern school, Perry Barr. The years that were to follow saw us cover so many miles together - happy days.

Two years ago my first book was published. Fearless Ghosts was all about the adventures we had together bunking into sheds all over the country in those far off days.

Now I'm off to revisit those sheds, yards, works, carriage sidings and marshalling yards in the company of other Fearless Ghosts.

Please travel with me via this book on another ride into yesteryear. Let us go back in time together. I'll try and stir your imagination and your own precious memories of those happy childhood days you spent racing and chasing after steam locomotives, diesels, electrics, experimental locomotives and other motive power.

The steam sheds and coal hoppers that stood towering over us youngsters are few. The ash pits have long been filled in. The odd turntable can still be found.

I'm about to embark on my own Magical Mystery Tour of Britain, 1998. Welcome aboard! I hope you enjoy your return to yesterday.

My old house at 12 Myrtle Grove, Pugh Road, Aston, Birmingham 6, no longer stands. The houses that once stood, oh so proud, down our grove were all knocked down some time in the Sixties. My late uncle Fred was the last person to leave. He stood at the top looking down towards the old brewhouses and with tears in his eyes, said: "What a shithouse."

I can still see the houses and their occupants. I can just about make out their faces. I also remember the local shops. The sweet shop was owned by Mr. and Mrs. Donnelly. The coal yard was owned by Dina - the last time I saw her was back in 1995. Mr. and Mrs. Barber had the off-license. Mrs. Mcleod owned the paper shop, and Mrs. Marriott the fruit and veg shop.

The old back to backs are just a thing of the past. The brewhouses, dollies, mangles, bed bugs and those flies stuck on the flypaper in summer are all just happy memories. The old palings are nowhere to be seen, the outside lavs where many a lady and gent patiently awaited their turn are visible only to me. Some of them brought their own paper, those charming ladies were more discrete, obviously. I remember the drawing pins that made a thousand holes in the ceiling from putting up many a Christmas trimming, and the colourful balloons we pinned to the ceiling.

Oh, how can I ever forget! The coal man, the rent man, tat man, milkman - God bless them all!

Sadly, we have to move on from my birthplace. The next port of call I'll be visiting is a modern Aston station, then under the railway bridge and up Holborn Hill. On my arrival, I smile at the high wall and the dirty old factory which still stands in its filthy condition. Flights still occupy the former steam depot area. Time for a photo.

We now move onto my second home of that era. The maisonnette that we occupied from 1960 to 1966 in Perry Barr. It's had a lick of paint since I last visited. The three tall blocks of flats still tower over the once clean and tidy area. The maisonnettes are now homes for the more wayward. This is my old house, 69 Bridgelands Way, Perry Barr, Birmingham 22.

A large, strong, metal looking object bars the way from any entrance into the old house. I'm peering through the dirty filthy windows, the smell of yesterday's pee still lingering in the air. The landing area is very close to my front door - in those days the landing would have been cleaned and scrubbed daily. The smell of disinfectant lingered all day long but you knew it had been cleaned.

I'm now standing halfway across the peck. I always took a quick glance back towards my house as once again I was no doubt heading off towards the bus stop for the bus into town. Once again starting off on another of my trips. It's a little sad that I'm looking back towards my house now. My folks, along with many a good neighbour, have sadly passed on.

I'm standing here some 39 years on and looking back towards my house. I know for a fact that my folks are still fast asleep in bed. So is my young sister, Sheila. I'm orf out on another spotting trip to? The bus stop that I stood at awaiting the Midland Red bus has gone. The company still have the odd bus or two knocking about. The Corporation buses are now called West Midlands Travel.

The first port of call today is 84E, Tyseley. The vast area still welcomes many an enthusiast. The large enclosed roundhouses are gone. In their place we now have a four-road maintenance shed. One section is for running repairs to electric locos. The second section is for diesel maintenance. The old diesel multiple units with their sickly exhaust fumes are very rare today. Personally, I hated them. The Staff Association club's still there. The office block now stands to your far left and another large maintenance depot stands close to the office block. A single Type 4 diesel, loco 40118, stands silently in the company of other locomotives. The chassis of steam locomotive 6201, a Princess class 7P Pacific, *Princess Elizabeth*, is here but other parts of this once proud engine are away undergoing overhaul at the East Lancashire loco works in Bury.

The Birmingham Railway Museum at Tyseley is under the watchful eye of Will Aitkins. He's partially in charge of the shop side of the business. Let's take a peep inside. What an Aladdin's cave we are entering.

The next depot is Saltley. It's still open. A three-road fuelling point is as close to the old coal hopper as I can recall. The amenity block is still there. The water tank is still in place. The vastness of the area that once housed three enclosed roundhouses has a variety of firms standing in its wake. It's very unfortunate that the sheds had to be pulled down, but I can still visualise them.

On arrival, I bumped into an old friend in the shape of Alan Mayher. He's an ex-fireman, ex-driver, and now a TCI. His work shift for this day was 06.00 to 18.00.

"Alex, I miss the old timers," he said sadly. "The saddest part of course is old friends who gave many years service to the railway and this shed in particular; they're no longer with us today. Many a good lad from the past is now just a photo in one's memory. One such person was driver Frankie Roberts. He had had his ashes scattered just behind the old Number Two shed. Silly really, but no-one knows exactly where the ashes fell. Another strange fact is no-one remembers who scattered them."

We were interrupted by a phone call. A class 47 had failed so Alan had to deal with that problem. I thanked him for his time and made my way out. Once outside, I casually looked around the area where the large enclosed roundhouses once stood. The turntables are gone, the "Duck" road and coal hopper are just about visible in my mind's eye. Some old brickwork remains on the site.

Today, new businesses occupy certain parts of the old loco. Wholesale greetings cards, Tacisa UIL and RS trade counter are among the many units that now stand on this massive former shed site. Suddenly, a local to Cambridge passes over the bridge. Years ago, it would have been a "Duck" or perhaps a Black Five. In the distance you can still make out the old station area. The many small avenues where the passenger and freight trains once ran through have been filled in. The brickwork still shows the entrance from the main road to the station at Saltley. In the old days the freight trains would line up as far back as Water Orton. I bet some train crews relieved the same train after their rest!

Before leaving I'll pay my respects to the late Arthur John Richards, an old driver. A small plaque affixed to the fuelling point wall is set beautifully between three small floral arrangements, the warm sunshine just lovingly touching it. The words written: "To commemorate Arthur John Richards." Try and see it.

Engineman supreme Lou Costello springs to mind. He brought the last steam loco into this shed way back in the Sixties. The reason for bringing the loco on shed was made up by him on the spur of the moment. I heard it was devilment. The old shed men reckon that they could bring a steam loco on shed for coal and water and be off the shed ready for its next turn of duty in less than 20 minutes. I for one believe every word.

I'll pause for a few seconds before we leave. My thoughts are on my first trip to this wonderful depot back in the early Sixties. I'll take a final, casual but sad glance at the area now. My private thoughts I know will make me cry. The thoughts of yesterday's train spotting trips that I happily made in the company of my two chums Melvin and David. Sadly, it's time we moved on - "bye."

I'm off to town now to take a look at what's in place of the old London and North Western shed at 21E Monument Lane. The six road straight steam shed and its tracks are not even visible from the point where I'm standing. There's no indication that a locomotive depot ever existed here.

I was told a story about this shed - its small signal box and how it was removed by an accident. A loco ran light from New Street station, came out of Holliday Street Tunnel and then over the points, making its way onto the shed area. Once it had been disposed of by the enginemen, it ran away and crashed into the side of the signal box. It destroyed most of the box on impact; I heard the bobby inside was only slightly hurt but for some reason the old box was dismantled after that incident. The old LNWR shed closed in 1962.

I only ever visited it on a couple of occasions and they were very early in my spotting days. However, in the years that followed I passed it on numerous occasions as I travelled further afield to other depots, like Wolverhampton, Crewe, Manchester, Liverpool, Carlisle and the best trip I ever undertook, Glasgow and Edinburgh. All that remains are some happy memories. The area is now a housing estate and a multi-storey car park but at least there is now a new shed just along the line at Soho, albeit an electric unit depot.

It's high time I moved on. I'm going to travel by train to Bescot. The eight road straight shed still stands. The diesel fuelling and inspection shed sits on the site of the old coal hopper. The turntable that was situated close to the Down station platform no longer turns those old steam locos, because there's no steam locos to turn - no turntable now either.

Class 8F 2-8-0 'Consul' No. 48507 on an engineers' train at Aston Junction.
(Alex Scott)

REVISITING OLD HAUNTS

I'm orf to another heartbreaking area - Wolverhampton. The three depots in that area were, in order of bunking: The great GWR shed at 84A Stafford Road, a terrific shed to bunk, another great GWR shed at 84B Oxley, and the LNWR shed at 21C Bushbury.

Stafford Road had a combination of straight sheds and an enclosed roundhouse. But before we revisit it, let's take a very painful look at the old, sadly run-down Low Level station.

I first came here way back in the early Sixties and you can guess who with, M. and D. The station opened in 1854, closed in 1972. Wolverhampton High Level was opened in 1852 and is still open but for me it has no character. The main line from Snow Hill to Wolverhampton Low Level had scores of people travelling along it but now its stations are just vivid memories. I'll just mention a couple: Hockley was a terrific place for train spotting, both passenger and freight hurried through at speed. At Smethwick, the Railway Carriage & Wagon Co. once manufactured Type 3 Bo-Bo diesel locomotives numbered D6500 - D6564. The firm also turned out diesel multiple units. They had a parent company in Gloucester which also built DMUs. I don't know when they ceased manufacturing.

It's raining heavily now so I'll skip going to the sheds for today.

It's a Saturday some time in June, '99. I'm standing outside the entrance

The rails are swamped by nature at Wolverhampton Low Level, left to rot for nearly 30 years. Will it ever rise again? *(Alex Scott)*

The grand entrance to Wolverhampton Low Level in 1999. It's seen better days - much better days. *(Alex Scott)*

to a small and compact little station. I turn into Borough Road, then first left into Wellington Road, left again into Shobnall Road. A small cinder path is situated on the right hand side of the road; this will hopefully lead me to a steam shed that once had two roundhouses. I'm now standing close to the former steam shed; there are no locos here today. On the site stands a factory, Premier Health. Another firm stands just to the left, New Images. A few yards away I can see a very pitiful looking ex-trailer; it must belong to a beer company. Where am I?

It's Thursday 17th June, '99 and I'm standing on the Down platform at Wolverhampton Low Level. Oh!, and it's not raining. There's an eerie silence about the place. I can feel a death-like atmosphere surrounding me. A closeness with the past is engulfing me.

On many an occasion I stood here awaiting my train home. The old station lights swayed gently to and fro in the darkness of both summer and winter evenings. I can hear muffled voices talking in the distance. I'm observing the railway staff as they prepare to meet the incoming service from Shrewsbury or Chester. The Birkenhead - London Paddington services were a treat to see.

The thundering sound of an approaching train hauled by a steam loco echoes around this once proud station. I remember on many a summer's day, whilst visiting this marvellous area, how the platforms were streaming with the sounds of children's feet as they followed the trains that came and went. The excitement that took over their young lives will never, ever be paralleled. The stories they told in class - in school - are light years away.

I have in my hand an old Locoshed Directory, 1961 edition. I'm now leaving the Low Level and taking the directory route to 84A Stafford Road. This will be another painstaking journey. I'm on board a local bus, No. 503. It's heading out of the bus depot towards Stafford Road shed.

I've alighted at the corner of Stafford Road and Bushbury Lane. There's an M. & B. ale house situated just a few yards from the bus stop, The Croft. It's a very hot summer's afternoon, too hot for a pint so I'll carry on with the business at hand.

The first depot I'll revisit will be Bushbury. I feel pretty confident a tale will unfold about the former depot since it closed its doors in 1965. Phew! It's a bloody long walk from the bus stop, but it's a lovely day for a stroll.

I'm just walking over the road bridge and just coming into view is a Bingo club, The Gala Bingo, in actual fact. Oh God! Once inside I spoke to the receptionist, Doreen. She was a very cheerful looking lady. I explained who I was and what I was doing here.

"My name's Alex, and I'm making enquiries about what was here after closure of the old steam shed." She looked at me as if I were from another planet - The Twilight Zone.

I stood patiently awaiting her first words. I thought to myself: "I hope she can talk."

Suddenly, she spoke: "No idea." A short pause then she spoke again. "The club's been here since 1991." A puzzled look came across her face. I knew she was reckoning up the years. "Yes, eight years we've bin here," she added.

An elderly couple approached the reception area, Bingo passes in hand.

"Hello," I said. "Do either of you remember what stood in place of this club prior to its opening in 1991?"

The elderly gent looked at me inquisitively, then answered: "Do It All. No, it was B.& Q. No, yes, Do It All." His wife nodded in agreement.

I was puzzled to say the least. Suddenly, a young employee came into the foyer. Doreen was quick off the mark and set about explaining who I was.

He glanced over in my direction, then asked for my phone number and said: "I'll give you a call in a day or two with the information you require."

I thought to myself: "What a nice boy."

He was just about to walk away when he turned and said: "There's a ghost who walks around the car park at night." He looked towards the TV monitor that hung in the corner close to the exit doors and pointed towards it. I could see it was monitoring the car park area.

"It was some time ago now. A railwayman was working along the track close to our club. They were laying some new concrete sleepers when, suddenly, a loud scream was heard. The sleeper had broken free of its chains and crushed the railwayman." He again pointed to the TV screen. "I've seen his ghost walk across the monitor many times," he added.

Doreen sat there nodding her head in agreement. "Yes, it's true. I've seen him as well," she said.

I said thankyou to one and all. Then I turned and headed towards the bus stop. I'd only been standing there a couple of seconds when a lady approached me. I remember her sitting quietly in the foyer.

"The club's built on top of the turntable. In fact the turntable is still there. They just filled it in with concrete," she said.

Then she hurried away. I wanted to ask her a few questions but at that precise moment my bus came. Once aboard, I sat quietly thinking about her statement. I alighted at Stafford Road. Then I walked along south Street into Jones Road, then up the pathway to 84B Oxley. The two enclosed roundhouses were closed to steam in 1967.

The sound of silence dawned on me as I walked towards the old shed area. It felt as if I was walking through a graveyard. I suppose in some ways I was. A Virgin set stood awaiting its next turn of duty.

On reaching the carriage repair shops I spoke to the young foreman, Dave Gough. I introduced myself to him, then asked about the old steam shed. It was a stupid thing to do because he was only a young man, but he may have some knowledge about the old shed.

"I haven't got a clue, Alex," he said, smiling. "However, I'll take you on a short walk around the area, but beyond that I can't really help you."

I stood there looking at the amenity block, it was as close to the old shed as I could remember. I said: "Thankyou," turned and headed towards Stafford Road via the shunters' cabin. An English Welsh and Scottish Railway shunting loco, No. 08698, stood silent outside.

Back to Stafford Road, and the old shed at 84A which once took up a vast area. I noticed that there were some newly developed buildings close to the

Locomotives on Oxley shed, 84B, 16th December, 1962:

Steam

GWR 57xx 0-6-0PT: 3605/89/9768
GWR 28xx 2-8-0: 3833
GWR Hall 4-6-0: 4959/5914/95/6937
GWR 56xx 0-6-2T: 5606/6631/44
GWR Grange 4-6-0: 6839/64/71
GWR Modified Hall 4-6-0: 6917/54/72
GWR 43xx 2-6-0: 7340
GWR Manor 4-6-0: 7806
LMS Class 8F 2-8-0: 48450/75/648
BR Class 2 2-6-0: 78008

Diesel

Type 4 'Western': D1004/37
BR 350hp 0-6-0 shunter: D3035/6/7/9/978

Total steam: 23
Total diesel: 7

former shed, one of them being a science park, a plaque stating that it opened in 1995. There was another large building situated to my right, close to Glaisher Avenue, a cul-de-sac - The Development Center. I think it was something to do with the unemployment service. Another business, European Platform Systems, was close to the shed area. There was still a vast amount of wasteland where the shed once stood - sad really.

Once again, I found myself standing at a bus stop and once again another city-bound bus approached. It was very hot and I was feeling rather saddened by what I'd seen, but then again I knew that my feelings were going to be hurt. I passed Molineux en-route to the city centre. The statue of the late, great Billy Wright stood proudly outside the visitors' end of this great stadium. I must get a photo on my next visit.

Locomotives on Wolverhampton Stafford Road shed, 84A, 16th December, 1962

Steam

GWR 'County' 4-6-0: 1013/23/4
GWR 51xx 2-6-2T: 4148/65
GWR 'Hall' 4-6-0: 4902/5919
GWR 'Grange' 4-6-0: 6803
GWR 'Castle' 4-6-0: 5026/47/65/7001/37
GWR 94xx 0-6-0PT: 8426/98/9435/75
GWR 57xx 0-6-0PT: 3778/9658

Diesel

BR 350hp 0-6-0 shunter: D3976

Total steam: 19
Total diesel: 1

I alighted just a short distance from the station. The train home departed at 15.06 and I arrived in New Street close on 15.26. I had enjoyed my visit to Wolverhampton, albeit at times it was a painful one, but I'm glad I went, it brought back some happy memories of the times I spent with M. and D.

I've started my day off with some pleasant thoughts about yesterday. Today, it's Thursday 17th June, 1999. Sadly, my mom's sleeping peacefully, so is my later father, he also rests with peace and tranquillity. I will be seeing them shortly. I'm looking forward to visiting Bognor Regis.

The 94 bus has just arrived at the bus stop. I'm off to Saltley first. It's very strange what I do each time I pass or visit this shed. I always look up towards the old number eight bus stop before I turn into Duddeston Road. It's a bit odd, I suppose - as if it's all done by a magic spell from yesterday.

Once on the site of this famous shed I get upset. I'm in the company of my two lost companions, Melvin and David. I can feel their presence with every step I take. Their ghostly figures are close by. I can hear their voices deep in my subconscious mind. I can hear Melvin's instructions to me: "Alex, you go and get those loco numbers there and those over there."

Suddenly, an eerie silence comes over me. I'm back to the real world. My short excursion into the past has slowly left me, albeit only temporarily.

Royal Scot class 4-6-0 No. 46132 *The King's Regiment, Liverpool* on Saltley shed on 11th June, 1962. This was the first picture I took with my Brownie 127 camera.

Locos seen on Saltley shed, 21A, and passing by on the main lines after school on Monday 11th June, 1962.

Steam

LMS Fairburn class 4 2-6-4T: 42053/82/225/30/84
LMS Fowler class 4 2-6-4T: 42410/6/22
LMS class 5 2-6-0: 42790/903
LMS class 4 2-6-0: 43012/7/44
Midland Rly. class 3F 0-6-0: 43242/389/453/521/583/99/665/80/7
Midland Rly. class 4F 0-6-0: 43940/51/63/79/4004
LMS class 4F 0-6-0: 44112/31/43/60/8/80/7/211/26/63/89/394/528/71/80
LMS class 5 4-6-0: 44664/776/7/812/919/20/44/5/65/5221/43/69/85
LMS 'Royal Scot' class 7P 4-6-0: 46103/22/3/32/7/57/60/2
LMS class 2 2-6-0: 46423/43/54
LMS class 8F 2-8-0: 48000/3/7/101/27/32/211/16/20/79/351/515/615/69/700
LNER class V2 2-6-2: 60848
BR class 5 4-6-0: 73013
BR 'Crosti' class 9F 2-10-0: 92027
BR class 9F 2-10-0: 92101/18/29/37/8/9/51/5/7/64/5/6/231

Diesel

BR/Sulzer 'Peak' Type 4: D6/28/39/123/8/34/53
BR 350hp(class 08) 0-6-0 shunter: D3168/248/576
LMS 350hp 0-6-0 shunter: 12042/4

Total   Steam: 97   Diesel: 12

Saltley depot, looking west in 1999 with Class 66, 60 and 47 locos present. The brick built three roundhouses closed on 6th March, 1967. *(Alex Scott)*

I'm in the company of an engineman, Mr Andrew Thomas. He's loaned me a new high visibility jacket so I can be seen as we go on a heart-warming tour of this homely ex-steam shed.

A handful of engines stood in the area: 08884 and 08905, 47331 - 348 - 703 - 712 - 772 - 788 - 839 - 844 and 58038. Three new Class 66 locos were also present: 66020 - 057 - 101. The last loco I witnessed was D9000, a Deltic class engine *Royal Scots Grey*. This was a real blast from the past. I just stood there in awe of this monster.

Andrew advised me about the workings of the Deltic: "Alex, it works the Saturday service from Birmingham to Ramsgate and return service."

I told him that some years ago I rode in the cab of a Deltic off Edinburgh Haymarket depot. "Thanks for the vest Andrew," Time to move on.

I walked the familiar walk up to Duddeston station. The old locomen's lodge house still stands. Sadly, it's in a very run down state. Duddeston station is no better. The carriage shed was pulled down and cleared away for new businesses some time in the Eighties. The wagon repair shops also closed sometime later. The shunters' cabin stands as a reminder of good times gone. The electric wires have also been removed - shocking!

The local electric service to New Street has just arrived. I'll hop aboard and find myself a seat. It's only a four-minute ride into town. As I arrive in the station, Class 47 No. 47812 stands at the head of a service to Liverpool. Another 47, No. 847, heads the Paddington service. A few local trains to Longbridge, Walsall and Lichfield occupy the concrete platforms.

Sadly, there's not a whiff of steam bellowing out of a Scot or a Jubilee.

There's no sign of a Semi or a Brit. Not even a Black Five, what a f****** shame. Anyway, I'm orf to Bescot now. The all-stations service is about to depart. I must say, I'm a little bit excited about the journey. If it were a steamer hauling the service, I'd be more than bloody excited. They could have laid one on for me, couldn't they?

My train is just passing the up ballast sidings. A single Class 08 shunts the yard, 08567. Another 08 stands idle close to the old stabling point, 08623. I can see a line of dead diesel locos on the far side of the down yard, a very interesting mixture - Class 47s, 20s, 37s and 31s. It looks like Death Row. Once upon a time, steam locos awaited their fate in similar fashion.

The locomotive depot has an interesting selection of working locos scattered around: 08542, 08920, 37047, 058, 693, 891, Class 47 47768 and Class 66 66013. On the left hand side towards the housing estate stand more derelict locos, Class 08s, 31s, 37s and 47s. God!, there must be several million pounds worth of rotting metal diesels, dying.

I'll alight at the station and take a quick photo of the old steam depot. I can see a couple of waggers sitting underneath the station canopy holding the new loco books in their hands. I can hear a little bit of their conversation - the usual topic, trains. Another local train, this time to Stafford. I'll get on board, then alight at Walsall - 66017 passes on a loaded MGR coal train.

The semi-fast back to New Street will be in soon. Time to stretch my legs. Christ, the train's approaching already. Ah well, let's get on board. The service runs via Soho Bank. Years ago a Britannia class loco would assist the heavy mineral trains up the bank from the Perry Barr side of the triangle. A 9F would assist from the Great Barr side. They don't need them now.

A glance at the old brick wall where 21E Monument Lane shed once stood and then into the smoke-free 1,744-yard tunnel into New Street station. A single Class 86 loco stands silently in the dock, 86207. Two other class 86s have brought in busy trains: 86229 on the Euston-Wolverhampton and 86247 on a return service to Euston. At one time a Class 08 had the station pilot duty but that's become another sign of the times.

My final shed of the day is one of my all-time favourites, 84E Tyseley. I'm being accompanied on this little memory jerker by my wife Carol and my 12 year-old daughter, Ashleigh who I'm meeting up with later to look for a photo location for the cover picture of this book. She loves the trains - the best part for her is writing down the different loco numbers. Her favourite locos are the shunters. I suppose it's because they're small like she is. What's on? 08631, 13029, the boiler of Castle class loco 5043 *Earl of Mount Edgecombe*. I don't think the funds are doing very well at all. Another steam loco celebrity, 7029 *Clun Castle,* is also here and 0-6-0 pannier tank 7760 is in steam, marvellous. Sheltering just inside the workshops we find a fascinating assortment of odds and sods. It looks like a Hall class loco

The old steam shed at Bescot still stands forgotten but the two-road diesel shed lives on, as seen here with Class 31s and an 08 inside. *(Stephen Chapman)*

from where I'm standing. There's a Western Region tender close by. "Sod it, someone's coming, I'm off."

On and around the turntable we find another assortment of goodies. An ex-Cadbury works loco, a red double decker bus from London, a single diesel railcar, and three old LMS coaches. There are chassis of different steam engines, one includes a Jubilee, 45699 *Galatea,* also two cranes, one a 75-ton Cowan & Sheldon and another smaller one loaded into a small

Britannia Pacific No. 70005 *John Milton* on Soho bank pilot duty at Perry Barr. *(Alex Scott)*

open wagon. A class 31, 31468 stands partly covered on the left of the turntable, along with Type 4 No. 40118. The sun's going down on another memorable day, time to say goodbye.

I'm looking forward to another day trip soon. My next port of call will be Stourbridge. If possible I'll pop over to Kidderminster for another trip down Memory Lane and to take a look at what's there now.

It's another super duper hot day. It's Wednesday 23rd June, '99 and I'm sitting on the local from New Street to Stourbridge. I only ever visited this shed once and that was on Sunday, 6th January, 1963. It was during that bad winter but I was still out and about collecting engine numbers. As if a few snow flakes could stop the Fearless Ghost. On the way from that once proud Snow Hill station to Kidderminster shed via Stourbridge I wrote down the following locos I had seen: 6866 *Morfa Grange*, 6986 *Rydal Hall*, pannier tank 4665, two very dirty Consuls, 48045 and 48478, a pair of D1000 class locos, D1006 and D1049, a single class 08 shunting loco, D3996 and finally, at New Street, a green Type 4, D229.

Anyway, we'll deal with Stourbridge first. On the shed and inside the roundhouse stood a grand variety of locos. They were mostly tanks, however there were several Consuls resting peacefully along with a pair of Granges and two Modified Halls. The depot was a mixed freight and passenger shed. The passenger workings included services to Worcester, Hereford, Snow Hill, Leamington Spa and the North Warwick line as far as Gloucester. The real bread and butter stuff was the freight, according to a chap I met while visiting the above area on Wednesday, 23rd June, '99. I'll hand you over to Mr Paul Williams whom I met on arriving at Stourbridge Town station. Paul now works in the ticket office.

"Alex, I was a DMU guard for a while. I remember those days with a fondness that even now I find hard to forget.

"The blokes that worked at the steam shed were second to none and the camararderie we all enjoyed held a certain bond between us. It was a real pleasure to come to work. And those glorious summer days working either a passenger service or a pick-up freight were so special, everyone thought they would go on for ever." I noticed a touch of sadness had come into Paul's words. He sighed for a moment, a half smile coming across his face. Then he continued: "The hustle and bustle about the everyday working was a real treat. I'd hurry to work and on my arrival my first act was to study the roster and the notice board. I enjoyed every single duty I performed."

After a short break, Paul continued: "Alex, I remember the last steam loco to leave the shed prior to its closing down sometime during the late 1960s. It was a 2251 class and its number was 3205. I stood there watching it slip out of the 28-road roundhouse, through the yard and out of sight into history. The loco was bound for the Severn Valley Railway. The old four-road straight shed was bricked up. In its later days it held railmotor units. It's all a little bit sad."

I could have stood there all day listening to Paul but I must pop orf and take a look at what's there now. I followed the directory instructions to the letter. However, I'd only got as far as the end of the High Street when it became very apparent that I was lost. I could not identify anything else after High Street. The last visit I made to this place was over 36 years ago.

Once again, I have the Good Lord looking after me. This time help comes in the shape of a very well spoken gentleman. "Can I help you?," he asks me rather pleasantly.

"Oh yes, I've lost a road," I advised him.

I notice him jokingly start to look on the floor then peer underneath his car. I laughed at his sense of humour. At this point he looked up at me, then said: "It's not under there."

"Which road have you lost?," he asked, smiling at me.

I glanced down at page number 71 in my directory, then looked up at him and stated: "Stourbridge Road!" I stood there staring at him as another part of his character began to surface. He looked up the High Street, then glanced down the High Street. Suddenly - and very slowly - he said: "There's two or three ways you can get to it."

A pause in the conversation fell momentarily between us. I awaited for another piece of useless information from this very helpful chap. I spoke first, saying: "I'm looking for the old steam shed that once stood near to the area where you and I are standing."

"Ah well, why didn't you say that in the first place? Follow me," he replied. We only walked about 15 yards under the road overbridge when he pointed out the site.

There now stood a variety of buildings. These included Kwik-Fit tyres, Arc Sports, Dana, a components factory and Jarvis Removals of Stourbridge Ltd. I noticed several other large buildings but I had seen enough. On my return towards the High Street, I came in contact with a gentleman of the road. He was sitting on a grass verge, sipping something out of a bottle. "Lucky sod," I thought to myself. I arrived back at the Town station and bade Paul farewell.

I boarded the single car unit and was soon heading back towards the Junction. On arrival, a local service to Snow Hill awaited me. Once on board I felt a touch of sadness come over me. Life goes on but I wish it was winter of '63. I wish I could be here trampling through the snow, shivering with cold, my nose running, my fingers covered with my mom's old thick brown gloves. I'd give my life up just to see it all one more time. Just to relive it all over again.

The train eased its way out of the station. The yard to my left was once filled to capacity with a widely varied assortment of mixed traffic. Now it was only a weed covered area. A rake of sky blue chemical tanks stood silent next to a bright yellow track maintenance machine. There was not a sole in sight, not even a squirrel or a cat trying to dodge the trains that once hurried through this area.

Locomotives on Stourbridge Junction shed, 84F, 6th January, 1963
Steam
GWR 28xx 2-8-0: 2885/3815/56/7
GWR 51xx 2-6-2T: 4140/68/5192
GWR 56xx 0-6-2T: 6609/46/67/78/83
GWR 57xx 0-6-0PT: 3659/4646/87/96/9613/4/24/46/733/82
GWR 64xx 0-6-0PT: 6403/18/24
GWR Grange 4-6-0: 6827/32/54
GWR Hall 4-6-0: 6925
GWR Modified Hall 4-6-0: 6986
GWR 74xx 0-6-0PT: 7430/2/5/41/9
LMS 8F 2-8-0: 48165/330/402/10/24/30/50/60/74/696/761

Total

Steam: 46
No diesels

I felt my eyes gently close. Then, into vision came so many happy thoughts. The memories of childhood long passed made me smile. If there had been anyone sitting by me they surely must have thought I was fantasising about goodness knows what. The peacefulness of that warm summer's afternoon was only disturbed by a very familiar sound: "Tickets please, all tickets and passes for inspection." I'm pleased some things haven't totally and completely disappeared.

The weather had been very kind to me as it was still very hot when the train pulled into the new station at Snow Hill. I just couldn't bring myself to get off there. There are two places that I often visit, Snow Hill and New Street. I'll be honest with you, it hurts me so much to look at the two stations, especially this one. I'll alight at Moor Street instead.

The original Moor Street opened in 1909. Sadly, it closed in 1987. The new station that runs parallel to the old one opened that same year. It took me a very long time to visit this once grand old lady. The station is situated on the other side of our city, and it's of Great Western origin. I, along with Melvin and David, only passed alongside it on trips to places like Banbury, Oxford, Reading, Swindon, Basingstoke, that great shed at Eastleigh of course, and the many London area sheds.

I know for a fact that it was once a very busy station, especially in the summer time when the excursions ran to romantic places down in Somerset and Dorset. The posters that tried so hard to attract holiday-makers to all manner of West Country seaside resorts were sprinkled like confetti on every available notice board on every station throughout the country. They were magnetic to all us kids. I remember times while stood holding my mom's hand how I would stare up at a poster, the colourful picture depicting some far off place in Wonderland. I also remember seeing some poor little kid being dragged away from his dream holiday by his mom who no doubt couldn't even afford to put food on the table, everlone take the bairns away for a day trip. A holiday was just a few seconds looking up at a poster on a station for some poor souls.

   Today, the old part is disused and surrounded by mesh fencing. I suppose no-one wants to get any closer than the fence. But I know a man who does, and did. It's overgrown like so many other discarded and decaying buildings. I'm sure I saw David Bellamy ambling through the undergrowth. Then again, maybe not. It's late afternoon but not too late to take a photo of this heart-breaking scene.

   Talking about heart-breaking situations, the station in those war-torn years was a very different place. The holiday posters had been replaced by war posters advising passengers about the war and to be careful what they said to others - "Careless talk costs lives."

   The saddest part of the station's duties must surely have been the evacuation of all those children. They crammed the trains so full. Each child had a small bundle of clothing wrapped in brown paper and tied up with string. A small box hung around their neck. I believe it contained information for those who were responsible for looking after the poor sods on their arrival at a million destinations. I bet it was a holiday camp to some of our fellow Brummies, but a hell hole to others. The stories were rife about the way in which some poor kids were treated. The police were often called to look for a runaway. Some made it back home, some came back to find nothing left. Their parents had been taken away from them. God, how I feel for them.

   I have never carried a handkerchief but I wish I had one today. I'll take a photo of the old station once I stop crying and sniffling like a little kid. It's time to head off across town and home.

   I've enjoyed my short but emotional visit to Stourbridge. The station at Moor Street will always be a special place to me, even if it only acts as a reminder of one better day. Talking of one better day, it's Thursday 24th June, '99, I'm sitting in my kitchen and reading through a copy of our local newspaper and guess what? I won't tell you. I'll let you read it for yourself. God moves in mysterious ways. Oh, go on, I'll tell ya. The Metro News has just reported that Moor Street will reopen some time in the future!

The depots and works I visited without pass or permit 1960-66

London Midland Region
1A Willesden*
1B Camden
2A Rugby* plus test plant
5A Crewe North* Works*
5B Crewe South*
5C Stafford*
5D Stoke*
6A Chester Midland
6B Mold Junction
6G Llandudno Junction
8A Edge Hill*
8B Warrington(Dallam)
8F Springs Branch(Wigan)*
9A Longsight(Manchester)*
9B Stockport(Edgeley)
9E Trafford Park*
9G Gorton* Works*
12A Carlisle (Kingmoor)*
12B Carlisle (Upperby)*
12E Barrow
12F Workington
12G Oxenholme
12H Tebay
14A Cricklewood
14B Kentish Town
14D Neasden
15C Leicester(Midland)*
15E Leicester(Central)
16A Nottingham(Midland)*
16B Kirkby-in-Ashfield*
16D Annesley*
17A Derby* Works*
17B Burton*
18C Hasland
21A Saltley*
21B Bescot*
21C Bushbury*
21D Aston*
21E Monument Lane*
24B Rose Grove
24D Lower Darwen
24E Blackpool
24F Fleetwood
24J Lancaster(Green Ayre)
24L Carnforth*
26A Newton Heath*
26B Agecroft*
26C Bolton
26D Bury
26F Patricroft
27A Bank Hall
27D Wigan
27E Walton-on-the-Hill

Eastern Region
30A Stratford Works
31B March*
34A King's Cross*
34E New England*
34F Grantham
36A Doncaster* Works*
36E Retford
40E Colwick*
41A Sheffield(Darnall)*
41B Sheffield(Grimesthorpe)
41D Canklow
41E Staveley(Barrow Hill)*
41H Staveley(Central)*
41J Langwith

North Eastern Region
50A York* Works*
51A Darlington* Works*
51J Northallerton
52A Gateshead
52F North & South Blyth
52G Sunderland
52H Tyne Dock
55A Leeds(Holbeck)*
55B Stourton
55C Farnley Junction
55D Royston
55E Normanton
55F Manningham
55H Leeds(Neville Hill)
56A Wakefield
56B Ardsley
56C Copley Hill
56F Low Moor
56G Bradford

Scottish Region
64A St. Margaret's
64B Haymarket
64C Dalry Road
65A Eastfield
       Cowlairs Works
65B St. Rollox
65C Parkhead
65D Dawsholm(closed)
65E Kipps
65G Yoker(closed)
66A Glasgow(Polmadie)
66B Motherwell
66C Hamilton
67A Corkerhill

Southern Region
70A Nine Elms*
70B Feltham
70C Guildford
70D Basingstoke*
70E Reading South
71A Eastleigh* Works*
71B Bournemouth
71G Weymouth*
71L Southampton Docks
72B Salisbury
72C Yeovil Town*
73A Stewarts Lane*
73C Hither Green
75C Norwood Junction

Western Region
81A Old Oak Common*
81B Slough*
81C Southall*
81E Didcot*
81F Oxford*
82A Bristol Bath Road*
82B St. Phillips Marsh*
82C Swindon* Works*
82D Westbury*
82E Bristol(Barrow Road)
82F Bath(Green Park)
82G Templecombe
83B Taunton*
84A Wolverhampton* Works*
84B Oxley*
84C Banbury*
84D Leamington Spa
84E Tyseley*
84F Stourbridge Junction
84G Shrewsbury*
84H Wellington
84J Croes Newydd
85A Worcester*
85B Gloucester(HortonRd.)*
85D Kidderminster
85E Gloucester(Barnwood)*
85F Bromsgrove*
86A Newport Ebbw Junction*
86B Newport Pill
86E Severn Tunnel Jn.
87A Neath Court Sart
87D Swansea East Dock
87F Llandore
88A Cardiff Canton*
88B Cardiff Radyr
88C Barry* Woodhams*
88L Cardiff East Dock*
89A Oswestry Works

Visited more than once

"LOOK EVERYONE, ALEX HAS COME TO VISIT US!"

I have a copy of the Great Britain National Rail Passenger Timetable, Sunday 30th May to Saturday 25th September, 1999, price £9. I'm smiling to myself as I skip through the various tables. I'm searching for a train to Tamworth, with a departure time of 08.10, Saturday service.

The new platform 7 at Birmingham New Street has changed beyond all recognition in comparison to the old platform that stood separated from platform 6 by Queen's Drive.

The Devonian from Paignton to Leeds runs at a different time now. In fact, it runs through to Newcastle. It departs Bristol Temple Meads at 07.04, arrives New Street at 08.40, departs at 08.45, arriving in Newcastle at 12.17. The service operating company is Virgin Trains. It's a High Speed Train and it doesn't stop at Tamworth, first stop Derby at 09.23.

The golden age of steam still lingers in the thoughts of many a grown-up kid. The Peter Pans of this world still live on. But the Jubilee class locos and the Scots that once pulled this long established train are just yesterday's memories for those who still can't come to terms with that final running of Britannia class loco *Oliver Cromwell* on 11th August, 1968 which spelt the end for thousands, no, millions of spotters.

On Saturday afternoon 10th July, '99 I was in the company of my wife, Carol, and my youngest daughter, Ashleigh. She's only 12 and a lovely little girl who loves the trains, albeit the diesels. We arrived at Tamworth Low Level at approximately 13.30. My wife parked the car and sat there reading while Ashleigh and I visited the many, many friends whom I had not seen since 7th July, 1962, some 37 years ago. We walked along the low level platform, then up a flight of steps to the high level. I held her hand tightly because she jumped as a passenger train flashed below us en-route to London.

We clambered down another flight of stairs which led to the low level platform, looking south. Our arrival coincided with another express hurrying through, this time heading north. Then another heading south. A local service passed above on the high level, it stopped momentarily, then moved slowly out of the station heading towards Birmingham. My eyes followed it until it was out of sight. At this point Ashleigh and I made our way through what looked like a training school for railway employees. I knew for a fact I'd been expected because the fence that separated the buildings and the school was lying face down so we could gain entrance to the "Field of Pleasure." Once inside, I felt an eerie quietness of reality. Not even a wasp or a bumble bee busying itself amongst the flowers and trees. The sun had been very kind to us. It shone beautifully down on us as if pre-ordained. In fact, the whole day had been organized for my benefit.

I stood there looking in all directions, only the passing of another express interrupted my personal vision of that July day in 1962. I can still see my two school chums, Melvin and David. I can see a thousand other boys in the field. They are still here with me today. We are standing shoulder to shoulder in a dream-like time machine. I can still see some boys playing footy, cricket, rounders, chase - some are just sitting reading their comics while others eat their lunch.

There were those who just basked in a life of uncomplicated situations. How childish we all were. How young our lives. But the lives we were leading were soon to become only a memory of days like these. I personally treasured every single trip I made to this place of undiluted freedom and pleasure. The trips I made in the company of Melvin, David, Spinner, Eamon, Nicky, Gerry and the three Smith brothers are so close that I can touch them.

The time is 14.50. Another local train passes over the high level, this time it's heading in the Derby, Nottingham direction. In the Sixties that would surely have been a Black Five-hauled train. Then again, it may have been a Jubilee or a Scot. The thought of a double header made my mouth water as I stood there looking back at yesterday's childhood spent in the lap of the gods who chose this place for us.

I said a little prayer for those who stood side by side with me on this most auspicious day in my life. Another express thundered through on the low level but my prayers were undisturbed. I felt tears running down my face as I knew they would at some stage during this visit. One last glance around this unbelievable area. One last smile at my friends then it was time to utter those hurtful words that I knew I would have to say: "Goodbye lads, God bless ya."

My daughter Ashleigh could see me saying goodbye because she could see me gently brushing away the tears. She walked towards me, then she stretched out her little mitt and placed it in mine. "Time to go Dad, can we take a look at the caravan park, please?"

I looked down at her through blurred vision and said: "Okay, let's take a look at the old caravan site." We returned to the car. My wife had her eyes closed as she was enjoying the short break after the drive from Birmingham to Tamworth via several shops. We took the short drive from the station car park into the old caravan park. I can't remember what the official name is for the site. I'm looking at my notes and I must admit I felt sure I'd written it down. Oh by the way lads, the cafe's gone, so has the old oak tree that once stood proud in the fields of pleasure.

Once we had arrived in the park, Ashleigh and I decided to take a look around the original train spotting area that I believe dates back to pre-war

Back on the hallowed turf of the Fields of Pleasure, Tamworth, where back in the early 1960s hundreds, no thousands, of boys pursued their favourite past-time - spotting steam locos on the West Coast and Birmingham-Derby lines that cross there. This is one of them - me photographed by my daughter Ashleigh on 10th July, 1999.

days. The water column no longer stands on the up side of the tracks. The water troughs have long gone, so have the lads. We bumped into an ex-Brummie, Mr. Sid Sargent. He was attending to the flowers in the garden of his new home. I introduced my daughter and myself to him.

Sid had this to say about the caravan park: "Alex, the wife and I moved out here just over nine years ago. We have observed many changes. One significant change has been the slow running down and clearing of the old caravans from the original section of the park. There have been additional homes built in the years that we have been here, some were built and completed only a few months ago."

Sid was just about to say something when a Freightliner passed over the high level. I could see him smiling to himself. "I've got used to it now, Alex," he said. "Now, where was I? Oh yeah, the local residents were up in arms a couple of years ago when it became known that the council were going to allow the Ashbury bypass to run through the site, but it never materialised.

"There was talk of the food giant Sainsbury's building a massive shopping complex near to the site. Once again, everyone in the area opposed it and as you can see, it was never built. I know for a fact that the plans have only been temporarily shelved. I think it's only a matter of time before they get their way. It could be weeks, months or even years, but they'll build it one day."

In the distance I could hear a diesel locomotive accelerating. Suddenly, into view came another Freightliner drawn by a Class 47, this time heading south. At this point, Sid and I shook hands. I said: "If my book Fearless Ghost The Return ever gets published, I'll bring you a copy." We shook hands again, then Ashleigh and I departed this beautiful, serene caravan park.

We walked back towards the parked car. My wife once again had her eyes closed as she rested before the short drive home. We eased our way out of the caravan park. I took one last look over my shoulder before we sped away. I felt a strange sort of inner calm and peacefulness come over me. "Goodbye."

One shed which closed many years ago, was obliterated and then made a kind of comeback, complete with its turntable on which is standing 'Warship' class No. D821 *Greyhound*. Where is it? Read on to find out. *(Stephen Chapman)*

WHAT'S HERE TODAY, SATURDAY 17TH JULY, 1999

The short drive to another depot that has been lost in time was once again taken with my wife and daughter. We are just passing a small but friendly football club on the left. I worked there a couple of seasons ago. They played West Ham in the FA Cup. The result on that day was 0-0 so I've given you a clue. I'll leave it up to you to puzzle out exactly where we are.

My wife parked the car in Kennedy Close. I noticed a chap attending his garden. My thoughts went back to Sid Sargent whom I met last Saturday doing exactly the same thing, gardening. The time was about the same as well. The sun shone brightly on the flowers that swayed gently in the breeze. I approached the gentleman who had no idea I was walking towards him. In fact, I think he was a little alarmed when I said "Hello." He spun around then, on seeing little Ashleigh, he smiled that grandad sort of smile.

"Hello, little girl," he said, still smiling down at her. "Where have you come from?," he asked her.

"We've travelled from Birmingham," she advised him.

"Oh, just to see me?," he asked.

Ashleigh looked up at him, then a girlish smile came over her pretty face.

I introduced Ashleigh and myself to him. he placed his tools on the floor near to his garage. At this point, I set about advising him of the reason we were in this area. "I'm here to take a look at what's in place of the old steam shed that was here in the Sixties." I also mentioned about the book I had written and the day and date coincided with my 51st birthday.

"My name's Joe Farmer," he said. "I've lived here since 1966, the year England won the World Cup. In actual fact I was on holiday with my wife. We were only there because the house wasn't completed until just after the cup victory. That's why I remember it so well," he advised me.

"Oh and I know all about this area and the steam shed."

"Lucky old Alex," I thought to myself. "Once again you've bumped into the right chap at the right time, in the right place."

Joe set about telling me all manner of stories. "Alex, I believe the shed closed in 1964. The area was cleared by a building firm, Fletchers of Kingswinford. They started the clean up and the building of those houses you can see from here between 1964 and 1999. Some are brand new."

I never asked him the price of the house, I thought it would be a little cheeky. He continued: "My house at Number two, was the last house built by another firm, Whiting & Dudley. The old chap Whiting had a large house built close to the houses he was building.

"There's a railway line that runs behind my house, it's part of the line that runs from Kidderminster to Bridgnorth, the Severn Valley line." At that precise moment a local unit ran past on the Birmingham-Worcester line.

"It's a lovely little football ground just over the bridge, have you been there at all?," he asked me.

"Yes," I replied. "I worked for a football club several years ago and some of us were drafted in to act as extra stewards for a big cup match."

"West Ham," he was lightening quick to say.

I smiled at the sharpness and the quickness of his answer.

"Do you know, Alex, when I was a kid I'd cycle from my house, up Mucklow Hill to Villa Park. In the bad weather I'd catch the tram."

Suddenly, I noticed the expression on his face change, for some reason he looked a little on the sad side. "Do you ever remember a player named Gerry Hitchins?," he asked me. I was about to answer when he said: "He was a lovely lad, a local lad at that. We attended the same school in the little mining village of Highley. We also played in the same school football team," he enthused.

I thought it best to say farewell at this point. He looked very unhappy now and I didn't want to add to the obvious sadness he must have been feeling when he spoke about his school chum, the late, great Gerry Hitchins. We shook hands and as I was about to walk away, he asked: "Have you got a camera with you?"

"Yes, I have as a matter of fact," I advised him.

"Good," he said. "Take a photo of me and the baby." The baby meaning Ashleigh. I took a photograph, then shook his hand again and we parted company.

"Come again," he called. I must admit, I felt a little bit upset by the conversation because I met Gerry after a team training session many years ago which at that time was held half way down Trinity Road, Aston, Birmingham 6. I only lived a five minute walk from the training ground. Whilst I was there I scurried after the balls when they went astray. I'd kick them back to the footballers. I was only about six or seven, so the balls didn't travel very far but I booted them as hard as I possibly could.

One day whilst watching the lads train, a ball ran close to me. I jumped off the fence and quickly gathered it up. For some reason I never kicked it. I remember one of the players walking towards me and I handed the ball to him. I remember his name and exactly what followed after that initial meeting as if it were yesterday.

The player was Gerry Hitchins. He took the old brown, laced up football from my tiny hands, then he ruffled my hair. "That's a good lad," he said. Then, he turned and walked back to rejoin his team mates. One day, I recall, after a training session, Gerry came over to the lads who were sitting quietly watching. He signed his autograph on bits of paper. We were all brushing shoulders with a real footy star.

In those days the team walked the short distance back to Villa Park. Some of us kids would tag along with them, they used to talk to us about the matches looming, some more important than others. Those who were lucky enough to be in their company just listened intensely to all the stories that were banded about. One by one, the lads all went their separate ways but I used to hang around for no apparent reason; I was just a little snotty nosed kid with nothing better to do. On one of those hanging around sessions, I remember Gerry coming out of the side entrance. He looked over in my direction, smiled, then climbed into his car. I'm trying very hard to recall what sort it was.

The colour was sky blue, but the model was either an Anglia car or an Anglia estate. I'll go for the estate. I watched him roll the window down, then he beckoned me towards him. "Do you want to earn yourself a few coppers?," he asked.

I was sitting next to him in his estate before he knew it. We drove off into the countryside. I remember arriving at a farm.

"Come on," he said. "Follow me." I trapesed on a few yards behind him. The next thing I knew, I was carrying all manner of farm produce, including fresh eggs and a variety of poultry. The colour red made me feel sick. I placed everything down in the back of the estate then turned for more and more poultry. At least the eggs were covered up in large covered boxes. We drove off and were soon cruising up the Victoria Road, Aston. Gerry stopped the estate right outside a butcher's shop on the left hand side looking up towards Six Ways. The swimming baths were almost opposite the small shop.

Once the estate had stopped, we both stepped out. Gerry went inside. I awaited any further instructions. "Right lad, bring it all in quickly," I heard a voice call. I was out of the estate in a flash, the goods were taken to the rear of the building via the front entrance just as fast. It only took me a few minutes to empty everything that had been placed in the boot. I returned and sat in the passenger side. I was looking out of the corner of my eye when I noticed Gerry reappear at the front door of the shop. He waved and then jumped back into the estate.

"Where do you live?," he asked me.

"Oh, ermm, Pugh Road. It's only a few minutes walk. I can walk home, you know."

At that point, he turned the estate round and dropped me off at the corner of Pugh Road and Victoria Road. "Thanks a lot, see you at the training ground tomorrow, okay," I said. I closed the door carefully, then I waved him goodbye. I watched as the estate pulled away and disappeared down the Lichfield Road.

I walked home feeling so pleased with my little self. I bounced into our house full of pride. Skint! But full of pride.

The next day I was there at the training ground before the players had arrived. One by one they turned up just carrying their boots and a handful of footballs. I spotted Gerry straight away, his blonde hair flowing from side to side, that child-like smile on his young face. He was great.

I ran different errands for him over the coming months. Some of them were just local, but towards the end of every week we ventured out into the countryside to the farm. Then once again we'd visit the butchers shop up Victoria Road. To this day, I don't know who owned the shop. I did hear that it was his father's shop but I can't swear to it. Obviously it must have either been someone in the family, a relative or a friend. I'm not going to say what he gave me in the way of a few bob; all I will say at this point is that he was very generous towards me. It was a sad day for me when I read about his transfer to an Italian club. I recall it was Torino. A very sad day for the Villa faithful as we all know.

As the years went by I grew up in the shadows of Villa Park. But a turn of events had me once again in the company of another great player. My family moved from Aston to Perry Barr mid-way through 1960. I accidentally bumped into Stan Lynn who had just moved across the city from The Blues to Villa Stan was famed for his penalty taking skills.

He had bought himself a paper shop in Perry Barr and how I bumped into him was truly accidental. I remember it as if it were only yesterday. It was very early one morning. I had acquired a racing bike from an unsavoury source and was whizzing up and down Birchfield Road at speeds in excess of 10mph. Not on the road, though - more on the pavement. Well I didn't want to get run over, did I? I was flashing past Stan's shop when the door

Locomotives seen passing through Perry Barr, 12th June, 1962

Steam

Hughes Fowler Class 5 2-6-0: 42837/926
Stanier Class 5 2-6-0: 42957/9/79
4F 0-6-0: 44301/58/444
Class 5 4-6-0: 44752/60/6/840/4/73/942/5038/52/9/64/410/8
Jubilee 4-6-0: 45560/722/33
Royal Scot 4-6-0: 46113/25/46
Ivatt Class 2 2-6-0: 46425/92
8F 2-8-0: 48042/149/718/33/47
7F 0-8-0: 49373
J72 0-6-0T: 68719
Britannia 4-6-2: 70025/6/42
WD 2-8-0: 90707

Diesel

English Electric Type 4: D214/7/30/93/322
Sulzer Type 2: D5011

Total   Steam: 40   Diesel: 6

opened and a bell inside jingled. Outside were batches of daily newspapers all stacked up nice and tidy. I hit the brakes so fast that I nearly flew over the curved handlebars. With smoke billowing from worn rubber, I came to a stand just half way across the main Thornbury Road.

I turned round and hurried back towards the shop. On arrival, I said: "Hello, good morning Mr Lynn. Ermm, can I help you with those heavy papers, please?"

Now Stan was a strongly built chap and the one thing I thought he would not require was a skinny, scrawny looking little shit like me helping him. But, to my total surprise, he said: "Oh, thanks sonny boy. I'll get them all lined up for my customers as soon as you've brought them all in."

I grabbed the first bundle, picked them up and then, nearly falling arse over head, I eventually found the counter. I returned for the next bundle, this time I made it safely to the counter; another trip and another trip and made myself laugh when I said, a little on the loud side: "Stone me, this is too much like hard work."

I remember Stan handing me a few mixed sweets. I said: "Thankyou" then stuck one in my gob, the others in my jeans.

Once again, I had the fortune to be in the right place at the right time. I ran some special errands for Stan and delivered a few papers when he had no-one else. He was another friendly and at times generous person. This lasted a few months but after a while other things came into my young life.

The years rolled on by. I could tell you a million and one stories about my life from the first day, way way back on that cold, miserable autumn night in September, 1948. The day, Saturday, time of my birth, 11.45pm.

On looking back on those somewhat mixed and emotional days, weeks, months and years, I recall reading about the late, great Gerry Hitchins passing on to another field of pleasure. I remember reading about his rise to grace, then I started to cry so I stopped reading. "God bless ya."

It's time to move on. My daughter and I have rejoined my wife in the car. We are now off to another great place off interest. One could say that our next port of call is world famous. This is another of those "where is it?" places. The sunshine is still with us as we make our way through the beautiful countryside.

VANDALS & CANNIBALS

We've had a little bit of trouble finding this place. However, here we are.

Oh God, talk about Break Heart Pass. This is all so sad. Whoever is responsible for the sheer destruction of this fascinating little station that once had a very busy work programme should be hauled off and flogged. Unbelievable! And they have the audacity to call it a modern railway.

Evolution, I ask ya! Evolution! The very word conjures up a myth so universal that another word even stronger must surely exist, even if it's only for people like me to live and die in, and then get the chance to see it and do it all over again.

God, let's hurry up and revisit what I can only describe as another return from grace to Mother Earth. Oh, and not a steam engine in sight. No, there's no trains running at this present moment, not even one awaiting departure from this fabulous scenic area. This place where I remember watching people enjoying a picnic close to the lineside as I looked through my carriage window on the several trips I made this way during those wonderful summer Sundays so many years ago.

The concrete platforms sit horribly on the former site of this old station. The through road has gone. The small signal boxes that were responsible for the line workings, the shed workings and loop sidings have all been dismantled. The platform staff, I have no doubt, if here today could have told a thousand, no a million, stories about their working lives.

Those who gained hours of pleasure from witnessing this one time busy station area would surely turn over in their graves if they knew what was here today. I remember visiting this one-in-a-million place when I was about twelve years old. Busy? Busy is not the word I would use to describe it. No, the word would be "non-stop!" It was endless, the amount of work this outlying station did. It was on the go 24 hours a day, Saturdays and Sundays included. The very thought just blows one's mind. The number of freight workings alone surely totalled tens of millions since the beginning in 1840. Passenger services possibly the same. I spent many happy hours here as a young boy.

It's time to take a look at what's here today. I meet up with a charming young couple who were reluctant to give their names, but they have lived in Scaife Road since 1995. "The estate was once called Hazel Croft Estate," the young lady advised me.

I said: "Thankyou," and took two photographs before I left.

UNCANNY TO ARRIVE HERE TODAY

Today, it's Saturday 24th July, 1999. It was on this day way back in 1964 that I arrived by train from Birmingham Snow Hill with my parents and my sister, Sheila, to a holiday resort in this area.

The resort was Tywyn. I recall the locomotive that hauled our train, D1684. We travelled via Wolverhampton and Shrewsbury where we changed trains. I believe we were hauled by a steam loco from there but I honestly can't recall the loco's number. At a guess I'd have said a Manor.

The total number of locos spotted en-route came to 48. I copped only six but what a fabulous variety I saw. Class 47s, 08 shunters, Halls, Granges, tanks, Consuls, Class 4 and 5 Standards, a couple of Manors, one single 9F and a Britannia, 70045 *Lord Rowallan*. No such luck today, sadly.

Today, I'm in the company of, no, I'm in excellent company. Once again, my wife's with me, and so is little Ashleigh who, incidentally, broke up from school yesterday so this is a nice little day trip out for her and a good start to the summer hols.

The time is 12.45, the weather, most excellent but before we look forward, let's take a glance backwards at what we saw when Melvin, David and I visited the area on two separate occasions in those hazy, crazy days of steam.

The first venture we made in the area of Shropshire and Cheshire was on a wintry Sunday, 16th December, 1962. We travelled from Snow Hill to Shrewsbury via Wolverhampton. The first depot we bunked was 89A Shrewsbury. The former GWR shed was a roundhouse and the ex-LNWR shed a nine-road straight shed. On that day, they had a grand total of 65 locos on. The large yard which was situated between the main lines that ran from Shrewsbury station towards Hereford was in constant use. There were several cattle roads where cattle trucks awaited departure to markets up and down the country. The railway staff took great pride and care when checking that all the animals were up-standing prior to the trains leaving. If an animal was down it created a massive problem not only for the poor animal but for those who would surely fall somewhere en route. The speed of these trains was limited to 45mph as this was a very valuable cargo.

We pushed on into a very charming little shed and its small workshops out at 89D Oswestry. We were actually taken to the depot by a chap who was going to work. In fact, he was a train driver based at the shed. We enjoyed the walk and the stories he told us about the quaint little shed. There were 28 on, I copped 26. Inside the works there was four, I copped three.

We caught the local service that took us down a very picturesque branch

45

line from Oswestry station to Gobowen. A small 1400 class 0-4-2T loco, No. 1432, pulled the one-coach train. I took a photograph but, sadly, it never turned out.

Once we arrived, we awaited another service to Wolverhampton where on arrival we alighted and bunked the shed at Stafford Road. Then we bunked Oxley. The two sheds were very bare, just a handful on each one.

The bad winter of 1962/63 was finally petering out by the time we made another trip in that area. It was on Sunday, 10th March, 1963. There was still snow on the ground in certain parts of the country, including Birmingham. However, the three of us were once again out and about. This time we were heading for Chester via Wolverhampton and Shrewsbury. No sooner had the train pulled into Chester than we were off and scurrying along the streets in the direction of our first shed, 6A Chester Midland. An LNWR shed, it closed in 1967. Next, we caught the bus out to 6B Mold Junction. This was an LMS shed which closed its doors to steam in 1966. Both sheds were a first time for me, the first holding 41 locos and the second 26. I copped 15 on 6A and 12 on 6B, not bad.

Locos on Chester Midland shed, 6A, 10th March, 1963
Steam
GWR County 4-6-0: 1016
GWR Hall 4-6-0: 5995
LMS Fairburn class 4 2-6-4T: 42229/36/40/7/70/681
LMS Fowler class 4 2-6-4T: 42366
LMS Stanier class 4 2-6-4T: 42441/63
LMS Class 5 2-6-0: 42783/2859/923
LMS Class 4F 0-6-0: 44461/78
LMS Class 5 4-6-0: 44844/5043/247/89/325
LMS Royal Scot 4-6-0: 46148/55/65
LMS Class 2 2-6-0: 46470/509
LMS Class 3F 0-6-0T: 47324/71/89
LMS Class 8F 2-8-0: 48349
BR Class 5 4-6-0: 73040/8/67/71
BR Class 4 4-6-0: 75024
BR Class 2 2-6-0: 78018/32/3
WD 2-8-0: 90216/643

Diesel
BR 204hp 0-6-0 shunter: D2388

Total steam: 40
Total diesel: 1

We were soon on our way to another first for me, 89B Croes Newydd. The depot was just a 15-minute walk from Wrexham General station but, no doubt, we ran and walked the route. In all honesty, I don't remember a thing about this shed. But there were 36 locos on, including 0-6-0PTs,   0-6-2Ts, three Consuls, four Class 4 Standards, a single Class 2 2-6-0 and two 2-6-4Ts. I copped 24.

The final shed bunked on that trip was 84H Wellington. This lovely, small two-road brick shed was planted beautifully on the end of the Up platform. The directions, if followed, took you on a short five-minute walk via a flight of stairs just outside the station entrance, then a left turn along the road that ran parallel to the line, another left turn and you were in Victoria Road. The shed entrance was on the left hand side just over the railway underbridge. We just walked off the end of the platform and within seconds we were writing down all the numbers of the 11 locos that were on shed. The single road coal hopper stood close to the turntable at the opposite end of the shed looking towards Shrewsbury. I copped three.

Locomotives on Wellington shed, 84H, 10th March, 1963
Steam
GWR 57xx 0-6-0PT: 3631/3704/76/92/4605/9639/741/74
LMS class 2 2-6-2T: 41201/4/41   Total: 11

Today, the three of us are travelling along enjoying another beautiful summer's afternoon. My wife's driving. Ashleigh has just spotted Burger King - that'll cost me a few minutes, I know. I'm reading out the directory route for the shed at Shrewsbury but, because Ashleigh interrupted me, we all missed the turn off that would have taken us into Scott Street. So, over the English Bridge, a nice little three-point turn, back across the English Bridge and right into Coleham Head. At this point we forked left along Betton Street, left into Scott Street via two railway bridges and, bingo, here we are nicely parked up in Scott Street which is virtually opposite Burger King.

"Look Mom, Burger King," Ashleigh kindly advised us.

"Yes, sweetheart, we passed it ten minutes ago."

Ashleigh thought it time to hide behind her mom's seat and laugh herself silly. The two-minute giggling session over, it's now time to see what lies on the land of the old steam shed.

Not a lot. I stood there looking at the vast wasteland when a chap approached me. He was carrying two heavy looking Safeway bags. I begged his pardon, then introduced myself and my daughter to him. I also explained what I was doing there. He stood there with his laden bags and within a minute told me about everything I could see.

"Now then, my name's Les Burgwin. The road running parallel to us is Old Potts Road, built in 1989. Cinema Cine World was built in 1997 and Burger King in '93."

He smiled, then continued: "Safeway in 1991, or was it '92, somewhere about there," he stated. "The Vetinary in 1995, The Jaguar, now that was built in 1998. On your left where part of the old steam shed once stood, they're building a bath showroom." At that point he added: "I must go, my ice cream's going to melt."

Ashleigh and I just stood there watching him toddle off with his shopping. We walked across the wasteland towards the running lines. A strange sort of circle had been made by someone. It was shaped like an old turntable without the tracks. I took a photo of the old semaphore signals that were in the clear position. Just then, a local from the Hereford direction appeared, then another unit flashed past going in the opposite direction. I noticed the small signal box just neatly tucked away almost under the road bridge.

One final backward glance before we left this once upon a time Great Western shed.

"Time for a burger, Dad?," Ashleigh asked.

"Got any money on ya?," I was quick to ask her.

"No. came the reply." It was up to muggins to put his hand in his pocket. My wife thought it very amusing that I should be spending my hard earned dosh. "A quid doesn't go very far today, does it?", I joked.

"You're not having a burger then, Alex," my wife quipped.

"It's high time we moved on to Wellington," I advised them both as they scoffed on their over-expensive burger, with chips and a bloody ice cream thrown in.

I must admit, it was nice and quiet for a change, instead of listening to them I had a peaceful few minutes to think about the next port of call whilst they were munching away on their scoff.

We arrived at Wellington as the ticket office was just closing, dead on 13.30. My wife parked the car up and left Ashleigh and me to go off into another wonderland. The shed, coal hopper and the turntable were still there - but only in memory, sadly. In truth, they had all gone. There was only a handful of people awaiting their trains to wherever they were going. Then, out of the blue, I heard an elderly lady say: "The train's late. Late again, it never happened in my day." Those who stood close to her smiled politely. A car arrived and parked up just outside the station entrance. A lady and a young child stepped out of the car, followed by a gentleman. I watched as he led them onto the platform. Momentarily, he returned to his car, then he returned to the lady and the child who were standing close to me.

"Excuse me," I said. He looked at me, then he looked down at Ashleigh. "I'm sorry to have stopped you, but are you a local person?"

"Yes, I am. How can I help you?," he asked.

I explained who I was and what I was doing in Wellington. I was about to continue my conversation when he said: "You're about a month too late."

A short pause while I thought to myself "What the 'eck's he on about?"

At this point he introduced himself to us. "Derek Elke's the name. I'm a local lad born and bread," he said with so much pride.

I couldn't wait to hear what he was going to say next. "Now look here, last month the town of Wellington celebrated its station's 150th birthday. We're all very proud of that fact," he advised me with words of passion. He turned and pointed towards W. H. Smith's. The shop stood out like a sore thumb at the opposite end to the area where we were chatting. "A model of the station was on display in the shop next to Smith's last month, it was bloody marvellous," he added.

"The queues went all down the road and back up again," he said with more passion in his voice. "Yes it was a grand sight you missed, lad, a grand sight." At this point he ruffled Ashleigh's hair and rejoined his family.

Now then, most people would have been satisfied with the information that they had been given, but not me. Off to Smith's we go. Once inside the shop, I approached a chap who was in conversation with his gaffer. I immediately introduced myself and little Ash. Mr Chris Harris, an employee at Smith's quickly advised me: "Councillor Gary Davies organised the event in the shop that lay between Smith's and Sent's." Chris continued his conversation by advising me on how best I could contact the councillor. He also mentioned: "The Horsehay Trust was involved."

I thanked him for all the information he had readily and freely offered. I looked down at my watch; it was time to depart, gracefully and politely.

Ashleigh and I were soon heading back to the car via one last glance at the station. What stories of great, no, immense interest could be told if only there was someone around from those days.

An end wall - all that remained of Worcester Works in 1999. On the left is the former wagon sheet warehouse. (Alex Scott)

WORCESTER, THE AFTERMATH

It's Saturday morning and once again the sun's shining brightly, and we're off on another trip down Memory Lane. Today, we're going to visit that beautiful town of Worcester.

The race track's just a short bus ride away, so are the shops that go hand in hand with most towns. Malvern, famed for its mineral water, is only a stone's throw away. But, before we set off, another glance back at those loco collecting days with Melvin and David.

Melvin would plan our trip to either Gloucester or Bristol via Worcester. His reasons were simple, this way we could see and hopefully cop a few more steam engines. I made two trips to this area but I have only one recorded and that was on a Tuesday, 25th November, 1964. I'd bunked off school for the day. I also recall it was a month in between my trip out to Swindon. The reason for my lack of trips had escaped me, but then it came to me - there had been a rail strike.

On the way to Worcester via New Street and Bromsgrove we saw 43 steam locos on the way and at the two sheds we passed, plus one single diesel shunter, D2240. It was allocated to 31B March in 1959, so how it found its way over here only adds to the intrigue. I remember taking three photographs, bunking the sheds, enjoying my lunch, and scoffing two thirds of my packet of Jammie Dodgers. No doubt I washed it all down with a bottle of Tizer. That was yesterday, however.

Ashleigh and I are standing on the site of the old loco. The three-road straight shed was a Churchwood design. The four-road shed that was once set in a triangle is long gone. The busy London Road yard has gone. The Hereford sidings and the North sidings are still partly in evidence. I recall sitting on an old wooden Post Office barrow with my lunch, books and pens all scattered about. The clank, clank, clanking sound of buffers crashing against each other as a heavy freight train departed one of the yards makes me wish it was still here today. Sadly - it's time to move on.

Ashleigh and I are in the company of Mr Liam Brett. Years ago he set up a tyre business close to the former workshops at Worcester. Liam had this to say about his first job at the age of 16: "I remember my father, Gordon Geoffrey Brett, had arranged for me to work in the sidings at London Road. The job was very hard, a gang of us raised every single track onto wagons. It took us months to clear the whole yard. It nearly killed me, I was only a strip of a kid."

Liam then pointed out what was here today. "In the vicinity of the old works are a couple of warehouses, one engineering firm, also a very interesting building that once housed the tarpaulins to cover wagons over with

It's a storage unit now."

All I could see spread around the works entrance was rubbish galore. I said: "Thankyou and goodbye," to Liam. We rejoined my wife at the station. I took one last look around the area before we all departed for some lunch.

Locomotives on Worcester shed, 85A, 25th November, 1964

Steam

GWR 16xx 0-6-0PT: 1634
GWR 2251 0-6-0: 2232/44/53/91
GWR 28xx 2-8-0: 2895
GWR 57xx 0-6-0PT: 3682/4613/9/50/64/8792/9680
GWR 61xx 2-6-2T: 6147/55/69
GWR 64xx 0-6-0PT: 6435
GWR Grange 4-6-0: 6813/36/7/47/8/58/77/8
GWR Hall 4-6-0: 5979/6930
GWR Modified Hall 4-6-0: 6967/7909/26/8
GWR Castle 4-6-0: 5000/7013
GWR 93xx 2-6-0: 7335
GWR 81xx 2-6-2T: 8104
GWR 94xx 0-6-0PT: 8415/9490
LMS Class 5 4-6-0: 44758/966/5289
LMS Class 8F 2-8-0: 48309/621
WD 2-8-0: 90220

Diesel

Drewry 204hp 0-6-0 shunter: D2240

Total Steam: 42 Diesel: 1

Ready to depart with an express to Paddington, Castle class 4-6-0 No. 7013 *Bristol Castle* **at Worcester Shrub Hill on 25th November, 1964.** *(Alex Scott)*

A DIFFERENT TYPE OF ECLIPSE

The world has been bombarded with all the hype concerning the eclipse - an historic moment that the world will quite rightly remember forever.
  It all took place on Wednesday 11th August, 1999. Okay, so the last time it happened was in 1929, 72 years ago. In a couple of days it will all be forgotten. There was talk of what would happen, could happen, should happen but in the end not much really did happen.
  "It's history, it's history," I hear everyone saying. However, there's all sorts of history. There's another piece of history a lot closer to home, that I suspect some of us have forgotten, whilst others no doubt remember with fondness.
  My week started off in a perfect way. On Monday 9th August, 1999 my wife drove my daughter Bonnie and her boyfriend Jamie to Butlin's in Skegness. They were staying in a chalet for a week. Ashleigh was also in the car. I just about managed to fit my slim figure into the front passenger seat. I couldn't resist the temptation of a ride out, especially as I'd tapped my wife up to drop me off in Netherfield, once the location of 40E Colwick, a fantastic depot.
  On noticing the sign for Colwick, Bonnie said: "Dad, we're on a holiday, not taking a trip down Memory Lane." She was quite right, of course, but we were passing it sort of en-route to Skegness. I just smiled and looked at her. Jamie had his eyes closed but no doubt his ears were open.
  At 11.30am, I was kissing my wife toodle-pip and saying goodbye to Bonnie, Ashleigh and Jamie who had suddenly woken up. "See you, Alex," he said as I was stepping out of the car. I waved to them as they pulled away. My wife and I had made arrangements to meet up at Nottingham Forest's ground at 6pm that evening.
  The first thing I noticed about the area I was standing in, was how busy it was. The next thing I noticed was a chap cleaning his car. I ambled over towards him and introduced myself: "Good morning, my name's Alex and I'm revisiting the area looking for the old steam shed at Colwick."
  "It's gone, oh yes it went a long time ago," he said. "There's nothing here now, except for an industrial estate, you know. MFI, MacDonalds, Allied Carpets, Kingdom Leather etc."
  I believed his every word. I said "thankyou" and departed.
  I took out my old directory and followed the route to the old loco. Once I'd arrived, it was just the way he had said. A large industrial estate stood on the site of the former 18-road shed of GNR origin. It was situated nicely between Colwick North Junction and Colwick East Junction, and Colwick North Junction and Netherfield Goods line.

The site of Colwick sheds in August, 1999, a retail park.
(Alex Scott)

Locomotives on Colwick shed, 40E, 31st March, 1963

Steam

Ivatt class 4 2-6-0: 43032/60/1/2/4/5/6/80/9/108/45/52/4/5/6/60
Midland Rly 4F 0-6-0: 43954/64
8F 2-8-0: 48505
B1 4-6-0: 61088/92/141/60/2/75/77/88/227/64/81/5/99/301/90
K3 2-6-0: 61943/82
O4 2-8-0: 63644/750/4/70/816/9/37/59/73/900
O1 2-8-0: 63589/92/615/52/63/89/768/863
WD 2-8-0: 90002/5/37/84/104/18/69/94/259/63/304/83/93/428/545/629/74
9F 2-10-0: 92177

Diesel

Drewry 204hp 0-6-0 shunter: D2235/301
BR 350hp 0-6-0 shunter: D3624

Total

Steam: 72
Diesel: 3

I only ever visited this shed on two occasions. One in the company of Melvin and David, the second and final trip in the company of Gerry Williams, Nicky Hand, Eamon Crawley and Spinner. On my first trip - 31st March, 1963 - I recorded on shed a total of 73 mixed locos. Strange, I only marked a few off. On my second - Sunday 30th August, 1964 - I recorded 78 mixed locos. I copped 35.

There was a tremendous variety of locos for us to feast our eyes upon.

Midland 0-6-0s, shunters, Thompson B1s, WDs, O1s and O4s, 9Fs, Consuls. But today, instead of locos stirring, only my memories were being stirred.

I managed to bunk a lift to Nottingham station. On my arrival I started to walk towards the old LMS shed at 16A. En-route, I bumped into a chap who was carrying his shopping. I was carrying and reading my Locoshed Directory when I came to a standstill whilst looking for Middle Furlong Road.

"Excuse me," I said. "Any idea where Middle Furlong Road is please?"

"You're looking for the old steam shed, aren't you?," he said, as if he had read my mind.

I smiled, then said: "Yes. It was here the last time I visited the shed, in 1966."

He smiled, then added: "It's long gone my friend. The shed closed its doors way back in 1967. The only thing that's standing there today is The Indland Revenue. It was built in 1994." At this point he stated: "My father, Mr. George Bromwich, worked at the shed as a cleaner in 1927. After a few years he moved to Swindon but because of the work reorganising he moved back to Nottingham prior to the second world war."

He took a deep breath, then continued. "He was made up in the late 40s but, due to ill health, he retired from the railway in 1960. The last job he had before finally retiring was at the coal yard weighbridge." He glanced at

Locomotives on Nottingham shed, 16A, 31st March, 1963

Steam

LMS Fairburn class 4 2-6-4T: 42140/61
LMS Stanier class 4 2-6-4T: 42587/9/628/36
LMS class 5 2-6-0: 42756/63/839/56/80/97
Midland Rly 4F 0-6-0: 43855/918/28/51
LMS 4F 0-6-0: 44047/132/9/68/84/201/15/48/59/84/304/472/6/532
LMS class 5 4-6-0: 44658/773/806/56/61/918/5046/185
LMS Royal Scot 4-6-0: 46101/65
LMS class 2 2-6-0: 46406/96
LMS 3F 0-6-0T: 47533
LMS 8F 2-8-0: 48119/84/201/18/77/315/72/490/614/39/40/47/748
LNWR 7F 0-8-0: 48954
LNER O1 2-8-0: 63687
BR class 5 4-6-0: 73135
BR class 2 2-6-0: 78013/20/1/9
BR class 2 2-6-2T: 84006
WD 2-8-0: 90221
9F 2-10-0: 92081

Total
Steam: 66
Diesel: 11

Diesel

BR 350hp 0-6-0 shunter: D3083/4/5/246/90/696/12050/1/96/7/8

his watch then said: "I must go, my bus comes in two minutes." He hurried away and out of sight.

The last time I visited this shed at Nottingham, I had left home. On the shed I recorded 14 diesels. I honestly can't recall if the two enclosed roundhouses were still intact or not. However, it was all very different one summer Sunday in 1964...... there were 74 mixed locos on shed. They ranged from tanks, Jubilees, B1s, 9Fs, shunters, Type 2 Bo-Bo diesels, Consuls, Black Fives, Peaks, ED5, and a handful of 0-6-0 4Fs.

What a great shed this once was. I crossed over the main road into the station and glanced quickly at the monitor for the Worksop train. The time was 13.15, the Worksop train departed at 13.20. I hurried along to the ticket office, purchased my ticket to Shirebrook - £4.20 Cheap Day Return. "Not too bad," I thought to myself.

I hurried down onto platform 4 where the train was just about to leave. "Time for a sit down," I thought to myself once on board. I have never travelled along the Robin Hood line before. Apparently it had only been open for about eighteen months to two years.

I arrived at Shirebrook spot on time at 14.03 and followed the directory to the shed at Langwith Junction. Once I'd arrived I was in luck. I met Mr. Ron Clarke who was foreman at W. H. Davies Engineering. The shed had two large buildings side by side. I had only visited this shed once and I have no record of it. Of Great Central origin, it closed in 1965.

I was just about to introduce myself to Ron when he spoke. "And how far have you travelled to visit the former steam shed?"

"Birmingham," I answered.

"They come from all over the place to see thee former steam shed. Come on, I'll take you round. Mind where you walk, there's all sorts of things going on in the area," he added. Ron pointed towards some old 100-ton oil tankers.

"We are taking on all measure of new contracts. Those tanks are going to be converted into covered aggregate wagons, some time in the year 2000 - or 3000," he said, tongue-in-cheek.

"Here we are lad, the old steam shed. There have been a couple of changes but the main building has not changed since it was built." He paused for a while, then made me smile when he added: "Long before I was born, I know for a fact."

I took out my camera, then asked his permission to take a photograph of him standing just inside the shed.

"Fine, fine, you take all the photos you need."

I took a single photograph, then we headed away from the shed area. Ron stopped, then we looked upwards. I could see a smile coming across his

Mr. Ron Clarke stands in the entrance to the old steam shed at Langwith Junction on 9th August, 1999. The two-road shed is now used as a wagon works by W. H. Davies and Ron is the foreman there. There was also a three-road shed but this was demolished some time after the depot closed in December, 1966. *(Alex Scott)*

Still stained with soot as its engine's used to be. The road sign says you're in the railway village of Langwith Junction, once the home of shed **41J.** *(Alex Scott)*

face. "I remember the day we pulled it down," he commented. "The original plan was to blow it up with sticks of dynamite. They were to be set at the base but we couldn't get permission. So in the end we pulled it's legs off and it just crumbled." He paused for a second, then removed his glasses. "It's all a bit sad when I recall the day we pulled the old concrete single-road coal hopper down in '66."

Ron then pulled out a clean looking handkerchief, dabbed his eyes and then replaced his glasses. I looked at him as he stood there trying so hard not to sniffle back the tears. "We should have left it standing as a monument to all those who once worked at this homely little shed."

I was still looking at him and thinking how sad his words were and how much it must be hurting him. He glanced down at his watch, then asked: "What time's your train home lad?"

"Fourteen fifty six," I answered him politely. At this point we shook hands and said "farewell." I took one final glance at the old steam shed building. Then I turned and headed back to Shirebrook station. I took a photo of the worn down area sign - Langwith Jct. A small church stood just behind the sign. "How apt," I thought to myself.

I enjoyed the slow walk back to the station. On arrival I just glanced at the newly built station that had replaced the former Shirebrook West station. I could still see remnants of the old platform that was now covered by the new one. The one time diesel depot still stood to my right but it too had closed. I did visit it in diesel days but that's another story.

At 14.56 my train arrived. I boarded and sat down. Time for a sandwich and a sip of pop before my next port of call at Kirkby-in-Ashfield, which was a five-road straight shed in '58.

The only time I ever visited this shed was back in the early Sixties. I was in the company of my two school chums, M. and D. We were eating our lunch in the waiting room at Derby station when Melvin decided we should nip over to Nottingham and bunk the sheds in the area. I sat on the train reminiscing, a smile on my face as my thoughts were on those great days of loco spotting. I was miles away when I heard someone on the train say: "Hurry up love, we're nearly at Kirkby station." I grabbed my small bag and as the train was just easing into the station, I took out my shed directory.

I followed the route to the letter, it's only a ten minute walk from the station to the shed area. I had plenty of time so I enjoyed the walk. On arrival, my heart felt a little heavy because, once again, it had all gone. In its place now stood a variety of carpet companies and other notable firms - Romo Fabrics, Astran Beds & Carpets, Trent Carpets, Action Wholesale Carpets, Hertland Waterproof Solutions, Midland Box Co. On the opposite side of the road stood a boozer, Low Moor Inn. An Esso garage was just a few yards away to my right. There were roadworks all around the area, on nearly every corner, in fact.

The time was just coming up to 15.35. My next train to Newstead was not until 16.16. I thought about walking the three miles or so to Newstead, then again I thought about waiting for the train. However, the good Lord loves me so I decided to walk. I know what you're thinking - "pratt." But, I had another idea in mind. A lift. Maybe some good old soul may give me a lift if they're heading towards Newstead. Yes, I did manage to persuade a chap to give me a lift, albeit by a very devious method, I told a fib.

The only words that were spoken between the two of us as we headed towards the area of Newstead was when I got out of his van and said: "Thankyou and tarrar." I closed the door and he drove slowly away.

The mile-long walk was a very pleasant one but the whole area seemed to be held in a state of silence. It was very eerie to say the least. The silence was only broken by the passing of an odd vehicle. I arrived at Annesley at 16.10. I gazed on the vast overgrown wasteland. There was no sign that a steam shed ever existed. The last time I came here it was on a Sunday, 30th August, 1964. I was with Eamon, Nicky, Gerry and Spinner. Today, I'm alone, just my thoughts and fond memories for company. So sad.

I stood on the platform at Newstead awaiting the 16.21 to Nottingham. The train duly arrived, I boarded and sat on my own. As the train departed the single line station, I began to reflect on my day in the Nottinghamshire coalfields. I conjured up past visions of an area so steeped in tradition. The guard clipped my ticket as the train eased into Hucknall station.

Locomotives on Annesley shed. 16D, 30th August, 1964

Steam

LMS 4F 0-6-0: 44112
LMS Class 5 4-6-0: 44717/843/6/972/84/5138/342/6
LMS Patriot 4-6-0: 45535
LMS Jubilee 4-6-0: 45735
LMS Royal Scot 4-6-0: 46103/22/5/50/65
LMS 8F 2-8-0: 48142/61/8/254/304/24/55/76
B1 4-6-0: 61061
WD 2-8-0: 90042
9F 2-10-0: 92011/4/32/3/5/43/68/9/71/2/3/4/5/88/92/4/5/6/105/32/54
Crosti 9F 2-10-0: 92027

Diesel

BR 350hp 0-6-0 shunter: D3087/246/659/12056

Total

Steam: 48   Diesel: 4

Two passengers alighted, one boarded, then the train slipped quietly out of the station heading towards the last one at Bulwell before arriving in Nottingham at 16.50. The train arrived nine minutes late and stood outside the station awaiting a platform. Suddenly, into view came the Inland Revenue building - a cross between a 21st century sports stadium and a space ship that had just landed. My thoughts quickly returned to the conversation I had had with that chap whose father had worked at 16A Nottingham Midland. He said the Inland Revenue was on the shed site. I was sitting with my back towards Nottingham station, so the building was on my right. I was trying desperately hard to picture the old steam shed and I knew for a fact that if I were to be facing Nottingham, the shed would have been on my right.

The chap had definitely got it all wrong. I glanced out of the carriage window as the train started to pull away from the stop signal. On my left, I could see a grey oblong building. The words Castle Park were written at the head of the building. I decided to investigate once I'd arrived in the station. On arrival, I pulled out my shed directory and followed it until I came across Wilford Road. Once again, I stopped in my tracks because I could not see Middle Furlong Road. On the site of the old loco shed stood a firm called Thomas & Betts. It was closed so I couldn't ask anyone about it. I also noticed one or two other firms close by, but again they were closed. I decided to leave the area and make my way towards the footy ground. I arrived at five fifty five. Within a few minutes my wife and my youngest daughter, Ashleigh, arrived. I was so pleased to see them that we all called into MacDonalds for a treat, on me you know - Mr. Big Spender!

The drive home was enjoyable because the clouds had disappeared and the sun was now shining brightly. My wife told me all about her day. Ashleigh chipped in and told me all about the rides she'd been on at the fairground, also how much of her mom's money she'd spent on amusements. We arrived home in darkness, about eight fifteen. Carol put the car away and I put the kettle on to make us a fresh cup of coffee. Then I sat quietly looking through my old train spotting pads from the early Sixties. According to my pad 1 visited Grantham on Sunday 31st March, 1963 along with Colwick, Nottingham and Derby shed and works. I also stopped off with the lads and we bunked Burton. On that day, we saw a grand variety of locos, the total came to a staggering 454. Unbelieveable! Today, none.

On Sunday, 11th August, 1968, the last standard gauge steam-hauled train on British Railways was pulled by Britannia class 7 locomotive *Oliver Cromwell*. The day was a momentous one to say the least. The Fifteen Guinea Special was very special. Today, that date has been eclipsed by a different type of eclipse. I listened to the radio and there was no mention of the end of steam. The TV companies never mentioned it either.

TODAY WE'RE IN CIDER COUNTRY

I only visited this depot on two occasions, and one was on a wintry Sunday morning, 20th January, 1963. The whole country was in the clutches of the bad winter of '62/63. But, I was out and about collecting loco numbers. My attitude then was the same as it is today - "sod it!" So, I'll look back and explain what happened on that Sunday morning all those years ago.

I had packed my rucksack with all sorts of goodies, my shed directory, pad, several coloured pens, sandwiches, sweets, a bottle of pop and, finally, a box of Jammie Dodgers. My mom always called me up at least an hour or so before I left home. The train departed Birmingham New Street station, platform 8, at about 10am, pulled by a Black Five, number 45150. It was no doubt covered in dirt - a thick layer of grime would have been part of its make-up.

As it thundered out of the station, I would surely have had my head stuck out of the compartment window. Once the loco and its coaches entered the first of several tunnels, I would have been engulfed in thick black smoke. I loved it. The train twisted and turned along the track like a snake as we headed towards a variety of local stations. Suddenly, I was looking out of the compartment window as the train raced down the 1 in 37 Lickey Incline. Then we flashed through Bromsgrove station, passing the old shed on our left at speeds up to 75mph. It was a great feeling as we whizzed past the signal box that was situated on the up platform. I just about managed to write down two of the six pannier tanks that were allocated to the shed, Nos. 8402 and 8403. The others were on banking duty but I missed them because I wasn't as quick as I should have been.

The train slowed down as we approached the junction that led us to Droitwich Spa station and then onto Worcester station. There were two buildings situated at Worcester, a four-road straight shed and a three-road shed. They were set in a triangle of the Worcester-Droitwich and Worcester-Hereford lines. There were several large sidings on the left hand side as the train approached Shrub Hill station. I remember even on a Sunday the yards were very busy marshalling the freight trains for departure on Monday morning. Unfortunately, the locos that were doing the shunting were hidden from view behind all the wagons.

We left Worcester on time and headed towards Abbots Wood Junction where we veered right towards the next station en-route at Cheltenham Spa. There was a small shed there at one time but I never visited it. Another double delight awaited us as the train departed for Gloucester, Walls Ice Cream had a factory almost on top of the junction. Then there was Tramway Junction. The first shed I passed was at 85C, Gloucester

Barnwood. The shed itself was a roundhouse. Next-door was 85B, Gloucester Horton Road, a straight shed.

Today, the Bridge Too Far connecting Eastgate and Central stations has gone. I walked it on a couple of occasions. The wooden boards creaked; I couldn't see much because the windows were covered in dirt and grime.

The train departed from Eastgate station in those days. Bristol next stop. On arrival I bunked Bath Road shed where there was only a handful of diesels on - three Hymeks, five North British and a single Warship. I was in and out of the shed very quickly because I'd timed my next service to my next depot with only minutes to spare.

I arrived at my ultimate destination just after lunchtime. This depot was situated at the south end of the station, access being by a small gate off the down platform. The shed itself was a very unusual design. It looked like a straight shed but in fact it was a reasonably large roundhouse. There were 38 steam locos on shed and 11 diesel locos. I copped 26.

Locomotives on Taunton shed, 83B, 20th January, 1963

Steam

GWR 14xx 0-4-2T: 1471
GWR 28xx 2-8-0: 2822/82/4/3857
GWR 57xx 0-6-0PT: 3659/69/736/4622/55/5798/7713/8783/9647/70
GWR 5101 2-6-2T: 4110/31/43
GWR 45xx 2-6-2T: 4593
GWR 61xx 2-6-2T: 6113/46/8
GWR Hall class 4-6-0: 4932/4/5992/6923/7
GWR Castle class 4-6-0: 7015
GWR 43xx 2-6-0: 7304/5/26/33/7
GWR Manor 4-6-0: 7806
GWR 74xx 0-6-0PT: 7436
BR class 3 2-6-2T: 82008/30/42

Diesel

Warship Type 4: D818/24
BR 204hp 0-6-0 shunter: D2140/1
BR 350hp 0-6-0 shunter: D4163/4/5
North British Type 2: D6333
Hymek Type 3: D7008/11/51

Total Steam: 38 Diesel: 11

Today, it's Sunday 22nd August, 1999. My wife and Ashleigh are taking a short break from the drive down from Birmingham. I'm standing in almost silence outside Taunton station. There are two taxis awaiting a possible fare to somewhere. Ashleigh has now decided to take a look around the old shed area with me. We are walking over the one-time heavily used tracks that are still visible, other parts are very overgrown. The oddly designed shed and coal hopper are gone, but some ash pits are still visible. A small single road wagon repair shop towers above us from the days of steam. Ashleigh is picking berries.

On our return to the car, I noticed that there were several bay platforms at this once busy station. The main line platforms are extremely long, as if they were designed to take on one, two or possibly three trains at a time. I can only imagine those heydays. The services ran to so many places that

Giving way to nature, the wagon repair shop that once formed part of the depot at Taunton. *(Alex Scott)*

Ashleigh on the platform end at Taunton. The wasteland behind her was once the engine shed. *(Alex Scott)*

62

an old timetable would surely be invaluable today. A variety of services ran to Bristol, South Wales, London, the Midlands and beyond. To the east, Chard, and to the west, Exeter, Plymouth, Penzance, Barnstaple and Minehead.

We are now leaving this very quiet area. Once upon a time it was all so different. One day in a history lesson, someone may tell the young boys and girls about an era long gone by.

We are now en-route to Torquay for a three-day break. My wife took a small diversion towards Exeter. On arrival, we parked up and she took another short break. I decided to take a quick look around the area. I noted only three locos in and around the station - a Class 37, 37714, a shunter, 08792, and a very clean Class 66, 66106 in the yard. The sun shone brightly as we made our way on to Torquay. The hotel was first class and we were in for a very enjoyable break, so we thought.

"Sunny Paignton," I hear you cry. I also hear you say: "There's usually some steam engines down there at this time of year."

Okay, okay, yes I did take a trip to see the locos on the small two-road shed. Yes, yes, yes, I did write them all down. A class 03 diesel shunter, D2192, was on shunting duty, hauling class 25 D7535 out of the shed. Later it also hauled out pannier tank 6435. In steam and about to pull out with the 14.00 Paignton-Kingswear service via Goodrington, Broadsands Viaduct, Hookhills Viaduct, Churston, Greenway Tunnel, Greenway Valley, Noss Creek, Longwood and finally Kingswear, was 2-8-0T No. 5239.

It hauled a rake of original GWR stock, including a well preserved Pullman observation saloon. I know that some of you have spent your holidays down here. I also know that there's usually another loco on parade, and of course you'll all be rather annoyed if I don't mention the fact. But I'm on holiday as well you know. All right! All right, so there was another small locomotive simmering in the station complex. Yes, it just happened to be a King class loco, No. 6024. Oh, and I know I'm a really decent chap for writing it all down for you lot. The King was on loan and due to work on the Dartmouth Regatta fireworks specials. And before you ask, no I'm not going all the way along the River Dart just to tell you about the ferry service across to Dartmouth. I'm off for a bag of chips, tarrar!

On Tuesday the weather was really bad. Rain had fallen throughout the night but I was not going to be beaten by a hurricane. So we all decided a trip to Plymouth was warranted. The rain was relentless as we made our way to the town centre. I know what you're all thinking. I know just what you all want to know. Did Alex get round the diesel shed at Laira? Hey, this the Fearless Ghost himself you're talking about. Apart from a wide range of GWR 125 trains being serviced, I managed to note several Class 08s there: 08410, 08645, 08648(stored), 08641(power fault.) I saw two 08s in

King class loco No. 6024 *King Edward 1* at Paignton on 22nd August, 1999. *(Alex Scott)*

another yard. That's it, bugger off.

The rain continued throughout Tuesday and through the night into Wednesday. We left the hotel at dinner time and headed home with the rain following us. My wife had promised to nip into Gloucester, but she was now tired from the drive, especially in the torrential rain that had fallen hour after hour.

We arrived home in Birmingham at approximately 16.00 hours. The short break was partially enjoyable for the three of us. I won't tell you how much money I spent, but it was way over £4. And that was including the hotel. I know what you're thinking - Mr. Moneybags.

Today, it's Saturday 28th August, '99. The three of us are popping over to Leicester for the day and whilst we are there we hope to do a little bit of shopping. My wife has promised to take me to visit one of the two sheds that were in this one-time busy area. On 15C, Leicester Midland, there were just four class 60s: 60066, 60081, 60085 and finally 60090. No. 66024 hurried through on a Redland stone train. A sorry looking 08643 stood derelict behind the main amenity block. There was no-one about to ask any questions concerning the shed. Once upon a time there were two turntables, a small one that turned the 0-6-0 freight engines, and the large shed that accommodated the 9Fs, Consuls, Standards, B1s and many, many others. The coal stage has gone and all that remains of the old shed is a small outer wall coloured a darkish white. The shed was a 32-road roundhouse, plus a smaller one at the rear of the amenity block. A large car park and part of the signal box occupy the area that this once great shed stood on.

I visited 15E Leicester Central on one occasion but I honestly can't remember it. We finished off the day at 2A Rugby. The shed, signal box and the testing house where I once noted loco No. 71000 *Duke of Gloucester* on test have long gone. The viaduct still stands idle on the old Great Central.

Locomotives on Leicester Midland shed, 15C, 4th November, 1962

Steam

LMS Ivatt class 2 2-6-2T: 41228/71
LMS Fairburn class 4 2-6-4T: 42184
LMS Fowler class 4 2-6-4T: 42331/3/4/8/55/61
LMS Ivatt class 4 2-6-0: 43118
Midland Rly 4F 0-6-0: 43876/969/88
LMS 4F 0-6-0: 44013/30/113/82/231/403/519/30
LMS class 5 4-6-0: 44811/5/43/61/5305
LMS 8F 2-8-0: 48179/445/666
Midland Rly 2F 0-6-0: 58138
LNER B1 4-6-0: 61095
BR class 4 4-6-0: 75055
BR class 9F 2-10-0: 92084/109/19/20/2
BR Crosti 9F 2-10-0: 92029

Diesel

Sulzer 'Peak' Type 4: D25/46/62/89/136/51/60
BR 350hp 0-6-0 shunter: D3787/8/9/90/1

Total Steam: 38 Diesel: 12

One day they will reopen it, you'll see. Engines in the area today consist of 09021, 66035, 37377, 37109 and 47476.

Loco number 90019 had just hurried through with a Euston-Manchester service. A million trains must have travelled underneath the once majestic roof of this lovely station. Sadly, nearly all the glass has been removed. Dirt and rusting metal have taken over the structure. Colourful green grass and weeds now wander free in most areas on and around the station - a modern railway they would have us believe. The shed was of LNWR origin and had 12 roads.

ALMOST TO THE DAY

On Sunday morning 18th October, 1964 I had travelled to Cardiff via Worcester and Gloucester. We managed to bunk 88L, East Dock. There were 41 mixed steam locos on shed. Cardiff Canton, 88A, had 60 diesels on. Cashmore's works had 32 mixed steam locos from all regions awaiting scrap, while 86A Newport Ebbw Junction had 40 mixed steam locos on, 15 Class 37s, a single class 47, a single Hymek and three Class 08 shunters.

On the way home and in the dark I visited the two sheds at Gloucester. The first was 85B Horton Road, a 12-road straight shed. The locos on ranged from WDs to pannier tanks, Consuls, Standards, Halls, Peaks, a 47 and a handful of shunters. Over at Barnwood, 85C, an old Midland roundhouse, was another excellent array of mixed traction. A couple of pannier tanks, a single Standard, two Castles, a Hall and finally, no doubt en-route to the scrap yards of Wales, a class U, No. 31868. The two depots were only a stone's throw away and on a Sunday they were full to capacity. I saw a grand total of 66, copped 14.

The connecting station at Eastgate was closed many years ago and the bridge joining it with Central pulled down. I gather it was one of the longest connecting bridges in the country, but don't hold me to that. The Central station still feeds Bristol, London and the Midlands, albeit by a different route. The main lines to Newport and further into South Wales are still very much in use.

Today I'm in the company of Carol, my wife, and Ashleigh, my youngest daughter. It's a warm, sunny afternoon, 16th October '99. The tracks are still evident at Horton Road. The single line maintenance depot lies decaying. The shed was pulled down some years ago after it closed to steam in 1964. Barnwood closed in 1964 too; all that's there now is wasteland.

I met a charming couple, Mr. and Mrs. Wyatt. They were sitting in a car close to the former depot at Barnwood. I struck up a conversation with them. I ascertained the reason for their presence in the car park. Mr. Mike Wyatt stated: "We are here for a wedding, they are holding the reception at The Irish Club." The club stood a few yards away in the distance. Mrs. Wyatt rolled down the window of their Merc. Leaning out, she added: "The young couple are Mr. Julian King and his bride to be is Miss Marie Daldry."

My wife and Ashleigh were taking a short break and tucking into their sandwiches. The weather had once again been kind to us. I bade Mr. and Mrs. Wyatt farewell and returned to our car. The trip home found me in sombre mood. My thoughts were on today and yesterday. I was trying desperately hard to show no emotion as we headed home, but my repeated thoughts of the trips out that M. and D. and I made throughout the Sixties were constantly with me.

Locomotives on Gloucester Horton Road, 85B, 23.12.62

Steam

GWR 14xx 0-4-2T: 1409/24/55/72/3
GWR 2251 class 0-6-0: 2232/45/53/3203
GWR 57xx 0-6-0PT: 3745/4696/9663
GWR Castle 4-6-0: 5000/14/99/7000
5101 class 2-6-2T: 4100/6/09/16/41/2/63/5173
GWR Hall 4-6-0: 5951/68/80/6951
GWR 43xx 2-6-0: 6304/30/65/81/7317/35
GWR Modified Hall 4-6-0: 6983/6
GWR 72xx 2-8-2T: 7204
GWR 94xx 0-6-0PT: 8491
LMS Class 5 4-6-0: 45268
BR 9F 2-10-0: 92239

Total Steam: 40   Diesel: 5

Diesel

Sulzer 'Peak' Type 4: D115
BR 204hp 0-6-0 shunter: D2137
BR 350hp 0-6-0 shunter: D3989/92/3/4

The remains of Gloucester Horton Road shed on 16th October, 1999. All that stood by then was a small shed for track maintenance machines but the tracks and inspection pits of the old 12-road shed were still there in the foreground. *(Alex Scott)*

67

THOUGHTS OF NAN AND GRANDAD

Today, it's Tuesday morning, 26th October, '99. The time, 08.30. Ashleigh and I are standing on a reasonably quiet platform at Birmingham New Street station. We're off to Blackpool for the day and the illuminations. In 1956 I stood as close as I can remember to this very spot. I had a small brown worn-out case at my feet. My Nan and Grandad were stood alongside hundreds of other passengers waiting for the train to Blackpool.

The illuminations, gosh! What a treat I was in for. A steam locomotive peeped out of the smoke filled tunnel. Everyone on the platform turned their eyes towards this sight of sights making that unforgettable sound as it huffed, puffed and hissed towards the platform. In robotic style, everyone bent down and grabbed their belongings, then stood up straight again. Within seconds of this beautiful loco with its thirteen or fourteen clean maroon and cream carriages coming to a gentle halt, it was a mad dash to grab a seat.

Even the poor old guard was overcome with passengers and their luggage, prams, pets and the odd lad holding fishing tackle for dear life. I recall it was standing room only for some folks who unfortunately couldn't get a seat, but no lady ever stood up in those days long gone by. Many a gent and all the kids gave up their seats for someone more deserved. Anyway, it was a bit of a lark chasing new found friends from one carriage to the other, and so on. Tripping over someone's case usually brought out a few well chosen words. The only time a kid returned to his mom and dad was for some scoff and a guzzle of Dandelion and Burdock. Then another disappearing act until Crewe.

The sight of Blackpool Tower in the distance as the train approached the North station was the talking point for the final part of the journey. On arrival, it was a mass exodus for the hotels, b. & bs., caravan parks, chalets or guest houses galore. The hustle and bustle momentarily over and, if luck had it, you were now standing with a family in the same b. and b. or hotel, chalet or caravan park reception.

What friendships and romances were struck up on a chance meeting. Jim, Bert, Floss, Rose, Joan and Bill, little Sally, David, Peter, Mary, Uncle and Aunt Tom Cobley. Once unpacked, the nearest ale house was on the top of everyone's list, followed by a bellyful of fish, chips and peas. Add to that a couple of rounds of bread and butter, a nice pot of tea and that set everyone up for the first night of several spent in and around Blackpool.

Talbot Road was situated next to the North station and with all its b. and bs., this was a favourite place for most people who came to visit this grand old lady of holiday resorts. I was a bit lucky because my grandad had a very good job, he was a van driver for Ansells Brewery. The main building was situated on the Lichfield Road and Park Lane, Aston.

I say lucky because we always stayed at a hotel. It was very posh and completely different from my old back-to-back down Myrtle Grove, Pugh Road. The staff in the restaurant were like whippets racing from one table to another, then back to your table with the Soup of the Day, your main course and finally your sweet.

"I know I am," I said when being handed my rice pud or apple tart and custard from a young girl. A smile would always come over her face and a touch of redness appeared within seconds of my smart Alex comment.

Tea time over and a pot of freshly made tea stood on our table. My grandad poured out a cup for my nan. I would be sitting quietly sipping pop through a straw. He poured himself a cup and silence fell between us. We would withdraw from the table and make our way down the front. I'd call into one or two of the thousands of amusement arcades. My coppers spent and it was soon time to find a friendly boozer, usually under the tower, or as near as possible.

The darkness of another encroaching winter's evening fell upon Blackpool, but that's what everyone wanted. The lights were switched on and what awaited me after my nan and grandad had had a few drinks was indescribable. I recall my grandad covering my eyes prior to the vision that came into view.

"No peeping," he'd say. Then it was a case of Alex in Wonderland. I've never seen anything like it in all my life and I've never seen anything like it to this day. The eighth wonder of the world, surely. The lights were magnetic. I was enthralled by everything I saw. Even the tower itself was lit up. The trams looked marvellous as they passed by in both directions. It reminded me of Christmas back home when the lights were switched on, but they were nowhere near as fascinating as these lights.

Every night, after a few drinks, my grandad performed the same act. I must admit, it was like being blind and then being able to see all before me at the same time. How strange?

We spent the week mostly on the beach, dipping and trying the fresh sea foods. The competitions along the front were a real eye opener. Knobbly knees, bathing beauty costumes, funny faces, anything the old MC could think up at the time when he had the crowds in the palm of his hand.

The week just flew by. Sadly, it was our last day at Blackpool. We were all packed and the short walk to the station was a slow one for me. I wanted to stay there forever. "Keep up, Alex," my nan kept saying. "Keep up son, we don't want to lose ya in the crowds now, do we?" The idea did appeal to me, but the sooner we were home, the sooner we could plan the summer hols of 1957.

The journey home was a sombre one for many a young lad and lass. The thoughts of friends made and perhaps lost only added to the heartache. Once you'd arrived in New Street, a quick trip over to your bus stop and you were back indoors within a few minutes. It was like a dream coming to an end. A week like the illuminations came and went with such speed that only those with a photographic memory could really recall every highlight in the stories and tales he or she told in class at school on a November Monday morning.

Sadly, today there are no steam engines, the carriages no doubt all scrapped or maybe some survived on private railways. The old New Street has long gone into the annals of history. The droves of people awaiting trains no longer exist apart from the usual early morning and teatime rush hour. My worn out case went with the miskin men years ago. Oh, my grandad went home in 1958. Nan joined him in '75. I do miss them.

Ashleigh and I will be visiting the area of my nan's birth en-route to Blackpool. We hope to pop in and see what's at some of the old steam depots now. My nan was born into a very poverty-stricken family way back in 1900 in a little village known as Burslem, Stoke-on-Trent, in the county of Staffordshire. We'll be there for two reasons. One to take a minute's silence. The other to visit the two loco sheds that stood close to each other when I visited them back in the Sixties.

Whoops, now then. Due to a power failure near Stoke we are unable to visit the area. The first train out will see Ashleigh and I heading straight towards Crewe.

The old six-road rebuilt steam shed at 5C, Stafford, closed in 1965. I visited this quaint little depot on more than one occasion. Today, the shed still stands but it's now occupied by the Palmbourne Industrial Estate.

The signal box at Madely Junction is still there. Sadly, the troughs have

The old shed at Stafford, closed 19th July, 1965, just before it was redeveloped as an industrial estate.
(Alex Scott)

gone. Approaching Basford Hall where 5B Crewe South was situated, half a dozen Freightliners are awaiting departure. A variety of traction is in evidence - class 86s, 90s, 47s and a single 08. There's also a wide variety of diesel traction decaying in and around the old shed area. De-ja-vous.

On our right, the old open-ended carriage shed is still intact. There's plenty of stock visible, including some GWR coaches, no doubt for charter specials. A Crompton had its nose just sticking out from inside the shed.

Mr. Mark Stevens, the depot foreman at Crewe Diesel Depot welcomed us with open arms. He also gave us a list of all the locos on shed. Over at Gresty Lane, the two-road Western brick-built shed had gone, but the track still lay firm.

Crewe North, 5A. I truly have no words to describe my feelings. We took a short walk to the old works entrance. Sadly, like most railway plants, it's gone. The entrance lay close to a small hospital - Safeway's is close by now. I remember a couple of ambulances were in the vicinity of the hospital and I, along with M. and D., visited this shed in steam days on many happy occasions.

Ashleigh and I walked to the Electric Depot. I noted a few on - class 47s, 86s, 90, 92 and some coaching stock towards the rear. The ABB works had some very special and topical visitors. The entire stock from the recent

Jubilee class 4-6-0 No. 45601 *British Guiana* **on Crewe South shed on 17th January, 1965.** *(Alex Scott)*

Crewe North shed was an exciting place occupied by big, exciting engines such as, above, Coronation class Pacific No. 46256 *Sir William A. Stanier FRS*.
Below: BR-built Britannia Pacific No. 70050 *Firth of Clyde* at Crewe North on 4th October, 1964, the same day as above. *(Both photos by Alex Scott)*

Locomotives seen at Crewe North shed, 5A, 15th July, 1962

Steam

LMS class 2 2-6-2T: 41211/20
LMS Fairburn class 4 2-6-4T: 42079/149/227
LMS Stanier class 4 2-6-4T: 42575
LMS class 5 2-6-0: 42781
LMS class 5 4-6-0: 44687/761/71/7/913/5184/6/243/83/370/91/413/46
LMS Jubilee class 6P 4-6-0: 45556/709/22/3
LMS Royal Scot class 7P 4-6-0: 46125/36
LMS Princess Royal class 7P 4-6-2: 46206
LMS Coronation class 8P 4-6-2: 46228/34/42/53/4
LMS Class 3F 0-6-0T: 47505
BR Britannia class 7 4-6-2: 70019/26/8
BR Class 8P 4-6-2: 71000
BR Class 2 2-6-0: 78030

Diesel

Sulzer 'Peak' Type 4: D2
English Electric Type 4: D321/36/41
BR 350hp 0-6-0 shunter: D3001
Sulzer Type 2: D5002

Electric

Class AL: E3004 /11/5/69

Total Steam: 38 Diesel: 6 Electric: 4

Paddington disaster was in for fine tooth comb research - shame!

We hurriedly made our way back to the station. Then we boarded the Cardiff-Manchester to our next port of call, 9B Stockport. The nine-road straight shed closed midway through 1968. I only ever visited this shed once. Next stop was 9A Longsight. This massive area is still massive. The large carriage shed still stands, the electric repair shops are still there. But, sadly, the LNWR passenger shed has long, long gone. Originally a roundhouse, but later a six-road straight shed was added in 1957 to accommodate diesels. Apart from 08721 and a solo class 86 there was nothing really to see.

Over at 8B Warrington Dallam, the shed was on the west side of the main line, north of Bank Quay station and the allocation on Sunday 23rd March, 1965 consisted of tanks, Black Fives, Jubs, Consuls, 9Fs and a few shunters. Today a modern warehouse stands on the site of the shed. It is said that the old shed walls still line the inside of the modern building.

We're on the 13.00 from Bank Quay to Wigan. Passing 8F Wigan Springs Branch we could see an abundance of decaying locos all around the recently-closed diesel depot that had long since replaced the old steam shed.

Because we were short of time, we only walked to see what was in place of the other shed at Wigan 27D. The six-road straight shed closed to steam in '64. I only visited it on one occasion and that was on Sunday 3rd February,

1963. The total number of locos on was 34, and they were mostly Fowler and Stanier tanks with a cluster of Standards.

Today, we bumped into Mr. Robert Dunn, steel erector extraordinair. I introduced myself to him and then set about explaining what we were doing here. He looked at me and Ashleigh for a while, then spoke saying: "You should have been here last week. You're a week late to see what we have done." At that moment he pointed towards a heap of railway track. "You're standing on it," he said, enthusiastically.

My vision dropped towards the area I was standing on. A bloody large, muddy area with a steel superstructure over me head. I had no idea what he was talking about and he knew it. A half smile came across his cheerful face. He took off his cap and pointed towards the outer section of the structure. I still hadn't a clue what he was trying to tell this thick head, namely me.

We were standing together, two perfect strangers, laughing in each other's company. The only difference between us was that he knew what we were laughing at and I didn't.

"You're standing on the site of the old steam shed." I jumped back a step then the feeling of standing on hallowed ground went through my mind. Robert continued: "We pulled up the remaining tracks only last Thursday."

He walked me and Ashleigh around the muddy area pointing to the ash pits as we covered the entire area. We walked towards another large building. As we walked, Robert announced that his partner for many years was a Mr. Simon Elpson. Apparently, Simon had some photographs of the old shed in his office and Robert felt he would be only too pleased to show them to me. However, Simon was out on site somewhere, so the photos weren't available because no-one in the office knew exactly where he kept them.

Ashleigh gave Robert our address and asked, if possible, could we please take a look at them and return them to him by return of post. Robert agreed to our request. We looked forward to them arriving. A friendly handshake and we departed. We had only walked a few yards when Robert called to us: "Oh, by the way, that's where the turntable was - and still is!" I could see him pointing towards a small car park and close by was a small plant nursery. We waved to him and again parted company.

A hurried walk back to the station and within a few minutes we were boarding our train to Blackpool. I noticed a single Class 37, 37263, waiting the road as Class 56, No. 56017, ran past us on a MGR coal train.

Preston station had 37612 running through on chemical tanks, 86244 and 37225 were in the sidings. The short journey to Blackpool was highlighted only by the semaphore signals from Kirkham, Poulton-le-Fylde, Layton and

Ashleigh and steel erector Robert Dunn on the site of Wigan Wallgate shed where a new warehouse was being built on 26th October, 1999, just a week after the track had been lifted. *(Alex Scott)*

Locomotives on Wigan, 27D, 3rd February, 1963

LMS Stanier class 3 2-6-2T: 40090/145/91/8
LMS Fairburn class 4 2-6-4T: 42297/9
LMS Stanier class 4 2-6-4T: 42473/4/94/551/5/7/69/92/621/4/41/2/4
LMS class 5 2-6-0: 42711/5/21/31/4/94/821
LMS 4F 0-6-0: 44240/464/86/544
BR class 2 2-6-0: 78042/61/2/4

Total Steam only: 34

the two boxes at Blackpool. Two coaches lay silent close to the site of the old Lancashire & Yorkshire eight-road straight shed, closed in 1964.

We had a very expensive but enjoyable day in Blackpool. Talbot Road held my inner thoughts for a while. My thoughts were of my nan and grandad, also of a little lad on holiday. Ashleigh cost me a mint but she's a grand little kid and priceless to me. A local unit took us to Preston, a 125 to Crewe, then class 37 loco No. 37415 on the last part of our journey home.

Thanks for the memories Nan and Grandad.......God bless ya.

THE FLEETWOOD MACS

Fleetwood station was set close to the steamboat pier. It was no doubt a classical one, with an air of regency about it. The glass roof surely sparkled and sunbeams danced to the sound of a humble lifestyle in those summer times when everyone knew their position in life, when respect, courtesy and the tipping of a gentleman's hat was all the rage. A fair maiden would smile that lost little girl smile and then go about her daily chores.

A single line ran from the station alongside the pier and many a coal truck was ushered towards the steamer that in its heyday must have taken a million and one holidaymakers, businessmen and day trippers across to the Isle of Man. What gaiety for those who could afford the trip. Once on board, they must have had one hell of a time drinking, dancing and making merry the moment. One can only conjure up all sorts of happenings of that time, its places and people.

On the left of the old station, a passer-by would no doubt have witnessed another elegant art being put into practice. The ancient art of crown green bowling. There were two greens close to the station and I can only imagine the tranquillity of the game being played so close to a hive of activity that was this famous fishing resort with all the hustle and bustle of life in those days that seem only like yesterday to some.

I salute those gentle folk who fished the waters for a living, to put food in the mouths of babes in arms. The young lads who stood alongside their fathers who in turn stood alongside their fathers before them. I wonder how many spent their entire working lives on the fishing boats and the railways. One could always make them out because they wore those black oilskin coats to keep themselves clean and dry. They felt compelled to look after the elderly and take care of all their needs because in the past they had been looked after, and one day when their time would surely be called, they knew in their hearts that they'd be looked after until the Good Lord called a name.

Sadly, I never saw the station or the pier because my one and only visit to Fleetwood was made in darkness on a Sunday morning, 28th March, 1965. When the coach with all those train spotters from in and around Birmingham arrived at the shed, we were very quickly ushered around by a loco driver; he whizzed us around the old L&YR shed in total darkness. The shed was coded 10C by the year 1963, and was still 10C in 1965. It closed its doors to steam sometime in 1966. On shed we eventually found a good selection of locos. Notably, eight Black Fives, six Consuls, four 2-6-2 tanks, three Jinties, two two-cylinder Stanier tanks, and finally three shunting locos. I copped six.

Today, the former steam shed no longer exists. In its place now stands part of The Lofthouse Fisherman's Friend Complex. The name Lofthouse brings a few footballing memories back. I don't know if it's a family connection to that great footballing son Nat.

Until recently, a single track still ran from the old station to the ICI works at Hill House. The trams still run from Blackpool to Fleetwood, single fare £1.20 to you - the Fleetwood Macs.

Locomotives on Fleetwood shed, 10C, 28th March, 1965

Steam

LMS Stanier class 4 2-6-4T: 42460/94
LMS class 5 4-6-0: 44729/982/8/5107/200/6/74/444
LMS 3F 0-6-0T: 47468/577/666
LMS 8F 2-8-0: 48211/73/377/413
LMS 7F 0-8-0: 49618
BR class 2 2-6-2T: 84011/6/8

Diesel

Yorkshire Engine Co. 0-4-0 shunter: D2860/1/7

Total Steam: 21   Diesel: 3

THIS COULD BE THE LAST TIME!

Once again I'm in the company of Carol and Ashleigh, and once again we are getting ready for another trip down Memory Lane.

It's a very frosty Monday morning, 27th December, '99. I have packed all our lunch away and we are now ready to leave. It's 11.40, the car rolled out of the drive with us all inside and sitting comfortably. We were heading off on another adventure.

The last time I ventured down to this particular area I was also in great company. Melvin, David and I had a great day's spotting at the two depots we visited on a summer Sunday, 19th July, 1964. We also bunked 15C Leicester Midland.

Today, we're off to March and Peterborough. We were enjoying our trip out until we arrived on the outskirts of Leicester heading for the A47 to Peterborough. We were just pulling away from a stationary position when suddenly, a young lad decided to walk across our path. He was pushing his bike and carrying a box that no doubt contained some brand, spanking new trainers that he had just bought from one of the stores on our left.

Ignoring all the traffic and the signals, he just ambled out in our direction and suddenly, he and his bike were partially entangled beneath our front wheels. Within seconds he sprang to his feet looking very shocked. I jumped out of the car and was soon enquiring about any injuries he may have sustained. "Are you alright lad?," I asked him.

"Ermm yeah, I'm fine," he answered with quivering words. At that point he ran his hands over his body and legs. Then he squeaked: "I'm a little bit on the lucky side, aren't I?"

I sighed, then added: "Yes."

A smile came across his face, then he ambled off.

I returned to the car and jumped in. My wife looked at me, then we drove away. It was some moments later when she enquired about the young lad. "Is he okay, Al?," she asked.

"Yeah, no injuries. He was just a little bit shocked," I answered. The rest of our journey was trouble-free and fairly enjoyable.

On our arrival at March, I was confronted by the same sight that I had seen when visiting other old depots from the golden age of steam. The two large signal boxes that controlled the two level crossings were still operating. A colourful assortment of wagons littered the small sidings. A very distinctive assortment of tracklaying machines occupied the down sidings between the two boxes.

The platforms that once echoed the passing of a thousand passenger and freight trains that ran through the station from Cambridge and East

Anglia, Peterborough, the North and Midlands, were silent. Today, all that remains of the two Whitemoor sheds are memories and a couple of tracks and wasteland.

I left the area with a heavy heart and the feeling of loss.

Locomotives on March steam shed, 31B, 4th November, 1962

LMS Fairburn class 4 2-6-4T: 42103
LMS Stanier class 4 2-6-4T: 42430
LMS Stanier class 5 2-6-0: 42945/78
LMS 4F 0-6-0: 44260/73/509/21/81
LMS Jubilee 4-6-0: 45582
LMS class 5 4-6-0: 44775/860/2/810/5004/56
LMS 8F 2-8-0: 48008/56/109/12/24/493/526/48/624/36/81
LNER V2 2-6-2: 60883/97
LNER B1 4-6-0: 61005/52/4/9/66/88/96/119/49/71/82/204/5/33/6/52/4/80/6/7/300/63/
    61373/8
LNER B16 4-6-0: 61418/38
LNER K3 2-6-0: 61817/80/6/90/915/7/42/54/63
LNER K1 2-6-0: 62042
LNER O1 2-8-0: 63687/725/80/803/6/59/68/72/87
LNER O2 2-8-0: 63966/85
LNER J20 0-6-0: 64690/1/9
Great Eastern Rly J17 0-6-0: 65541
BR Britannia 4-6-2: 70000/1/6/8/9/10/1/3/34
BR Class 5 4-6-0: 73171
BR Class 4 4-6-0: 75043/55
BR Class 4 2-6-0: 76031/2/3/4
BR Class 2 2-6-0: 78022/5/37
WD 2-8-0: 90042/296/423/587/665
BR 9F 2-10-0: 92183/201

Total: 106   Another 55 mixed diesel locos on the diesel depot.

We drove to another great shed in the area. I was lucky to bump into Mr. Arthur Denton. He was cycling past our parked car with a lot more awareness than the young lad we had bumped into some hours before. I approached Mr. Denton and explained my reasons for being in the area.

"My name's Alex Scott and during the early Sixties my friends and I visited the depot on two occasions. I've returned to find out what's on the site of the shed here at New England."

A broad smile came across his elderly face. He climbed carefully off his bike, smiled another one of those great grandad smiles then to pointed to a large Royal Mail building. "That's it, sonny boy, that's what's there now."

I was just about to say thankyou when he added: "I started my working life as a 14 year-old railway porter. Once I had reached my twentieth birthday I took up shunting duties in the old Westwood Yard. In 1954, I worked as a guard at the old freight depot at New England. After closure, I moved back to station duties. Then, in 1995 I had to retire due to ill health."

Suddenly, a touch of sadness came into our conversation when he concluded: "Son, a lot of old timers are sadly no longer with us."

I held out my hand and he shook it. I really felt sad myself after our short but informative chat about the old days. I watched him cycle away, then I hopped into the waiting car and we headed off in the direction of the station. On arrival I just glanced around the area and wrote down a couple of locomotives that were stabled close by, 08714, 08569, 66003 and 66076. A passenger service to London King's Cross was announced. Silly really, I was looking for a steam-hauled train, perhaps an A3, A1 or even an A2. The thought of an A4 had me sniffling. Instead, 91019 hauled in the Great North Eastern stock. I stood and watched it depart, then we all departed.

The journey home was a sombre one for me. My thoughts were on the two

Locomotives on New England shed, 34E, 4th November, 1962
Steam

LMS Class 4 2-6-0: 43067/81/2/8/146
LNER A4 4-6-2: 60003/7
LNER A3 4-6-2: 60050/107
LNER A2 4-6-2: 60513/23/33
LNER V2 2-6-2: 60841/5/58/66/80/1/93/906/12/4/56/61
LNER B1 4-6-0: 61073/122/74/207/50/70/2/82/302/64
LNER K3 2-6-0: 61864/906
LNER K1 2-6-0: 62070
LNER N2 0-6-2T: 69504/20/3/9/46/83/93
WD 2-8-0: 90015/31/50/73/96/106/46/51/349/428/54/514/659/96
BR 9F 2-10-0: 92034/5/7/8/40/1/2/4/146/69/78/81/8

Diesel

English Electric Type 4: D342/8
BR 350hp 0-6-0 shunter: D3446/8/50/88/629/4075
Brush Type 2: D5645

Total
Steam: 71
Diesel: 9

trips that the lads and I had made way back in the Sixties. We arrived home and once inside I cooked us all something a little bit special. Chicken in brandy sauce with mouthwatering Jersey Mids. It was just my way of saying thanks to my wife for taking me.

On Wednesday morning, 29th December, '99, my wife and I for some strange reason woke up fairly early. Once out of bed, I peeped through the curtains and once again it was a very cold and frosty looking day.

"Al, do us some breakfast and I'll take us all out for the day. Where do you wanna go?," Carol asked.

In a flash, I answered: "Chesterfield."

The three of us had a full breakfast then set about packing some lunch and within an hour of waking up we were on our way to Chesterfield.

The first of the three sheds in that area was out at 18C Hasland. Sadly, it was wasteland. No sign that a shed had ever existed. Over at 41H, Staveley(GC), the scene was just as sad - wasteland again. The final depot in that area was 41E Staveley Barrow Hill. Ashleigh and I ventured carefully around the shed. How refreshing to meet up with some hard working volunteers in full flight working on a variety of steam and diesel locos.

Once again, luck was with us and we soon bumped into a great lad in the shape of Mr. Steve Rodd. He gave us a conducted tour of the shed. Ashleigh took two photos, one of Jubilee class locomotive No. 45593, name *Kolhapur*. The second photograph was of an industrial engine, No. 11682. Steve Gave us a full list of all locos on shed. We had a brief chat and he explained how every project needed contributions totalling thousands of pounds. We departed and headed home just as darkness started to fall. Once indoors, another super duper meal was cooked by yours truly.

Locomotives on Staveley G. C. shed, 41H, 3rd March, 1963

Steam

LMS Jubilee 4-6-0: 45576/683/725
LMS Royal Scot 4-6-0: 46151
LNER B1 4-6-0: 61027/47/1139/51/4/66/228/66/312/73
Great Central Rly O4 2-8-0: 63656/85/92/705/6/35/72/4/81/827/41/913
LNER O1 2-8-0: 63571/96/630/46/78/784/95/899
WD 2-8-0: 90005/337/522

Diesel

BR 350hp 0-6-0 shunter: D4030/1/52/64/8/93

Total
Steam: 37
Diesel: 6

Locomotives on Staveley Barrow Hill shed, 41E, 3rd March, 1963

Steam

Midland Rly 0F 0-4-0T: 41531
Midland Rly 1F 0-6-0T: 41804/75
Midland Rly 4F 0-6-0: 43882
LMS 4F 0-6-0: 44010/066/71/089/113/28/9/74/205/12/65/87/404/26/37/75/521/35/68
LMS 8F 2-8-0: 48026/9/144/50/1/79/89/99/216/331/41/508/15/33/9/765
WD 2-8-0: 90202

Diesel

BR 350hp 0-6-0 shunter: D3707/4045

Total
Steam: 40   Diesel: 2

A WET AND WONDERFUL DAY IN SOUTH WALES

I was working at Beaufort Sports and Social Club on Sunday evening, 2nd January, 2000 when a friend of mine called in to see me.

"Happy New year, Alex. Oh, and by the way what are you doing tomorrow?," he said.

"I haven't made any plans to go anywhere," I was quick to answer.

"My son Anton and I are off to Pontypridd. They're at home to Newport in a league match," he added.

"A trip down to South Wales. Mmm," I thought to myself. "Interesting."

I knew that George and his son Anton were regular visitors to Pontypridd and they were sort of ticket holders. I must admit I've never really been interested in rugby. However, I did pick up some rugby programmes when I visited Partick Thistle's football ground some years ago. Funnily enough, I recall giving them all to George because he was interested in them.

We stood in silence whilst I contemplated a trip out. "I'll be sitting near the bar. If you fancy coming with us tomorrow, let me know before I go home. We'll be leaving reasonably early and we usually arrive back home around the nine thirty area," George finally concluded. At that point, he walked away from where we had been chatting. My thoughts were on all the depots in that area and whether I could get around to visiting some of the old sheds in the time available.

It was some time later that same evening when I approached George just to inform him about going with him to South Wales. George was also interested in railways, especially the old steam engines. He bought my book Fearless Ghosts, and I recall him mentioning some of the sheds he'd bunked when he too was a spotter in steam days.

I had to word my reasons for going with him very carefully as I didn't wish to appear uninterested in his interest which was rugby. George was drinking with some friends. I awaited a lull in their conversation then nipped in. "George, mate. I'd love to come with you tomorrow but I feel a little perturbed about my reasons for joining you," I said rather nervously.

A smile came to his face, then he stated: "We're off to the match, Alex, and you can go off and write about the old steam sheds."

I was a bit surprised by what he had said. "Alex, when I bought your book you told me that you were about to embark on a fact finding trip to see what's there in place of the old steam sheds now. Do you recall our conversation on that point?," he asked me.

I thought for a while, then answered: "No."

"No matter," he said. "We'll drop you off at some advantage point and we'll meet up later in the evening. We're in no rush to get home, I'm not due back at work till Wednesday," he joked.

"Thanks George, I really appreciate your offer. What time shall I call at your home in the morning?," I asked him.

He thought for a moment then stated: "Nine. Yes, we'll leave about nine."

I left him drinking and chatting with his friends. I spent the remainder of that evening picturing and puzzling out all the old steam depots that I, along with Melvin and David, once visited. Thoughts of manholes in Newport came flooding to mind.

Ashleigh and I arrived at George's house at approximately 08.50. Within a few minutes we were heading off to Pontypridd via the M5. George and I chatted about most things en-route to South Wales. The match, football, cricket, railways and the weather that at the time looked to be on our side, well at least until we reached Gloucestershire. From there the rains fell and never stopped. It was still raining heavily when we arrived back home in Birmingham after nine pm.

The silence that had momentarily broken our conversation on the day's proceedings was interrupted when George commented: "Alex, look out of the window and tell me what you see."

I peered out of the left hand side window and all I could see was open space and wasteland.

"Any idea where we are, Alex?," George asked me.

"Not a clue George to be perfectly honest with you," I answered.

"We are passing over the area where the old steam shed used to be at 86E Severn Tunnel Junction," George stated. The windows were rain sodden and because of this I couldn't make out any of the old landmarks - the station, the up and down marshalling yards, the shed.

The shed closed to steam in 1965. Originally it was a four-road straight shed, but because the area had become so busy, two further roads were added. I only visited it once and that was en-route to Birmingham after a brief visit to Newport on Sunday evening 13th January, 1963. The total number of mixed locos on shed came to 59. I copped 34.

The following locomotive depots that Ashleigh and I revisited via train, bus, the gift of the gab and walking on a rainy day in South Wales on Monday 3rd January, 2000, are as follows:

Ebbw Junction 86A. A couple of tracks are all that remain of the enclosed roundhouse with its two turntables. The BR Staff Association club still stands to the rear of the old GWR shed and a new housing estate has sprung up.

Cardiff Canton 88A. The depot closed to steam before Melvin, David and I arrived on Sunday afternoon, 27th January, 1963. Today, Ashleigh and I

bunked the diesel depot and found a fine assortment of locos on.
Neath Court Sart 87A. This shed was an enclosed roundhouse and the

Locomotives on Newport Ebbw Junction, 86A, 13th January, 1963

Steam

GWR 16xx 0-6-0PT: 1614/8/53
GWR 2251 0-6-0: 2209/18/39/43/3201/11
GWR 28xx 2-8-0: 2839/49/85/91/4/3805/7/16/24/33
GWR 42xx 2-8-0T: 4227/65/6/83/97/9/5213/7/27/8/9/34/6/8/55/9
GWR 56xx 0-6-2T: 5664/70
GWR 57xx 0-6-0PT: 3624/62/3700/6/14/72/4611/27/57/71/9/5722/7736/8751/81/ 9616/9644/62/7/718
GWR 43xx 2-6-0: 6325/40/90
GWR 64xx 0-6-0PT: 6412
GWR Grange 4-6-0: 6800/50
GWR 72xx 2-8-2T: 7217/9/23/4/32/3/8/40/5/53
GWR 94xx 0-6-0PT: 9444
WD 2-8-0: 90066/474
BR 9F 2-10-0: 92006/222/5/6/9/30/2/5/8/49

Diesel

BR 350hp 0-6-0 shunter: D3748/812/3/15/6/9/22/4128/76/7/8/80/2/4/5
English Electric Type 3: D6742

Total

Steam: 86
Diesel: 16

David Burrows and Castle class 4-6-0 No. 5051 *Earl Bathurst* at Neath Court Sart shed on a Sunday in spring 1964. The loco still runs to this day but I haven't seen David since we left school shortly after this visit..*(Alex Scott)* three of us bunked it some time in the spring of '64.

We also bunked Swansea East Dock, 87D, which was situated in the town's dockland area. The second shed bunked was out at Landore 87E. Sadly, all I have in the way of proof are several photos I took of Melvin, David and myself. The pad in which I recorded what was on Landore and other depots we bunked in Liverpool, Manchester and Yorkshire was lost long ago.

The Metal Box company now occupy the former depot at Neath; they also have a sports field there. On the site of Swansea East Dock, Sainsbury's have a large store. British Telecom have a building in the same area, and the Bank of Wales have their offices there. A diesel depot occupies the land at Landore. It comprises a four-road maintenance shed plus a four-road fuelling point. At Malphant Sidings only a small rake of Post Office vehicles awaited their next run up to London on the Monday-Friday service. Diesel shunter 08795 was on shed along with 47815.

Barry shed and the old graveyard of future dreams at Dai Woodham's was next on our list. The six-road straight shed had gone, so had the yard. A car park partially occupied the shed area. The last time we visited this sad looking area was way back on Sunday 7th February, 1965. The shed housed seven class 37s and a single 0-6-0 shunter, D3437. The yard held a fantastic array of mixed traction totalling some 90 engines.

The old steam shed at 88B Radyr was bunked by the three of us again on Sunday 27th January, 1963. It was opened in 1931and was a GWR standard type shed with four roads. It closed to steam in 1965. On our only ever visit there, we noted an all-tank allocation of 46 on and three diesel shunters. I copped 41. The shed remained closed for a number of years before a garage took up residence. The PAD, Pre-Assembly Depot, supplies the railway with track. In the old days of steam, Powell Duffryn cleaned the locos. A brand new housing estate is now being built in and around the old locomotive depot.

The last shed in the Cardiff area we bunked was over at East Dock, 88L. The shed was an eight-road straight shed. Its locos were of mixed traction - Castles, Halls, Granges, Manors and 9Fs. Some locos had transferred from Canton on its closure. On the day we visited there was an all-steam assortment of 48 locos. I copped 21. Today, in it's wake and in darkness, is a variety of restaurants and shops. Harry Ramsden's has a fish bar there and a science park was recently opened.

The last shed Ashleigh and I visited was over at Newport Pill, 86B. The depot, once owned by the Alexandra Docks & Railway Co., once consisted of a very long two-road straight shed made out of brick. It closed its doors way back in 1963. On 13th January, 1963, some days prior to its closure, we saw 18 steam locos on and 18 diesel shunters. I copped 33.

Above: Melvin(right) and David with former Cardiff Railway 0-4-0ST No. 1338 while bunking Swansea East Dock on a Sunday in spring, 1964. *(Alex Scott)*

Below: Same day, same place with David and me(left) and BR Standard class 4 2-6-4T No. 80133.

86

It's way after teatime and it's bloody cold, dark and we're soaking wet but, in the area of the old steam shed, we were lucky to meet ex-railwayman Mr. Alan Norman. He explained what's there now: "The old Octopus Bridge, Braithwaites Engineering, Rowcard Engineering, oh, and the old shed was referred to as Pill Gwently. Of course, it was later known as Newport Pill."

We departed the area after Mr. Norman and I shook hands and bade each other farewell. The number 15A bus took us back to the bus station in Newport.

George and Anton collected us close to six pm. Within half an hour we were sat down in a Burger King restaurant scoffing burger and chips, followed by a carton of Coke - my treat for taking us on a journey filled with so many happy memories.

We arrived back in Birmingham just coming up to 9.15pm. I had had a great day travelling down my own Memory Lane. Pontypridd had won their match and they remained top of their league so, all in all, everyone enjoyed the day. I'm looking forward to another trip out down Memory Lane, although at present I don't have a clue as to where I'll be going.

Locomotives on Newport Pill shed, 86B, 13th January, 1963

Steam
GWR 57xx 0-6-0PT: 3674/705/4639/73/8702/9664
GWR 42xx 2-8-0T: 4233/8/50/1/3/4/9/64/71/6/80/94

Diesel
BR 350hp 0-6-0 shunter: D3807/9/10/1/20/4001/2/11/2/125/6/7/70/1/2/3/4

Total Steam: 18 Diesel: 17

WITH TEARS IN MY EYES

I only ever visited this depot on one occasion. I recall travelling alone and sitting at the front of a grimy DMU. If my memory serves me it had a yellow V outside on the front end of the driving cab. The unit travelled via Nottingham and I arrived in bright sunshine on Sunday afternoon, 31st March, 1963. The depot closed some time in '63 so I was a little on the lucky side to find it open on that particular spring day.

Once the train had stopped, I was off and with my shed directory in hand I ran very child-like out of the station, turning left, then underneath the railway lines, then a hard left and I was soon scampering around the eight-road shed. Within about 12 minutes of my arrival, I was boarding another unit back to Nottingham. There was a nice mixture of steam and diesel locos on the shed, 44 in fact. I copped 16 steam engines and three diesel shunters. What depot did I visit?

There are several things that come to mind. Firstly, I remember the coal hopper - it towered high above me. Monolithic sums it up. There was an eerie silence about the area, a sort of calmness surrounded me as I whizzed round the shed. I don't expect anyone to believe my next statement, but it's true.

Once back on the platform, a unit to Nottingham awaited me. I placed my rucksack in the first seat behind the driver's cab. I recall him sitting there awaiting departure. I had my head out of the window and, strangely, I knew I'd never visit this depot again. My eyes were fixed on the towering coal hopper. The signal to depart came from the guard who blew on his whistle. There was a sudden rev of engines and we were slowly pulling out of the station.

It was magical to say the least. Suddenly, my right hand rose upwards and I started to wave the depot goodbye. I was still leaning out of the window and waving as the train hurried away and on to Nottingham. It was as if the coal hopper had never been there, all of a sudden it was gone. My heart felt heavy as I sat down and looked out of the window as the train sped on.

Once I'd arrived in Nottingham, I set about the business of collecting locos. The bus to 40E Colwick where there was a fine selection on which totalled 79. I copped 35 and they were mostly steam. In and out as quickly as possible. Next, over to 16A Nottingham Midland. Another cross section and, oddly, 79 on. I copped nine. It was time to board another unit to Derby. Once again, it was a case "in, bin and gin." The shed and works had a grand total of 96 on and I copped 11. Time once again to catch another local unit home, passing Burton and Saltley in darkness.

Locomotives on Derby shed, 17A, and Loco Works, 13th March, 1963

Steam

LMS Fowler class 3 2-6-2T: 40026
LMS Stanier class 2 2-6-2T: 40157
LMS Fowler class 4 2-6-4T: 42335/9/92/422
LMS Stanier class 4 2-6-4T: 42472/500/85
LMS class 5 2-6-0: 42784
Midland Rly 3F 0-6-0: 43637/58/69
LMS 4F 0-6-0: 44049/54/176/214/62/333/94/545
LMS class 5 4-6-0: 44664/757/5274
LMS Jubilee 4-6-0: 45561/7/610/2
LMS class 2 2-6-0: 46402/95/7/9/500/2
LMS 0F 0-4-0ST: 47000/3/6
Midland Rly 3F 0-6-0T: 47236
LMS 3F 0-6-0T: 47272/325/441/7/53/534/629
LMS 8F 2-8-0: 48124/53/89/98/286/399/500/654
LNER B1 4-6-0: 61084
GCR O4 2-8-0: 63620
LNER O1 2-8-0: 63725
BR class 5 4-6-0: 73143
BR class 4 4-6-0: 75041/2/51/6/9/62/4
WD 2-8-0: 90012/153/249/471/566/665/82
BR 9F 2-10-0: 92085/101/13

Diesel

Sulzer 'Peak' Type 4: D33/42/7/64/70/1/3/8/81/2/4/5/92/4/111/3/7/20/7/30
BR 204hp 0-6-0 shunter: D2377/8/80/2/3/6
BR 350hp 0-6-0 shunter: D3245/372/862/4
Sulzer Type 2: D5010/31/78/80/141/86/7/8/9/92/3
Birmingham RC&W Type 2: D5393
Brush Type 2: D5836
English Electric Type 1: D8011
Fowler departmental 0-4-0 shunter: ED3
LMS 350hp 0-6-0 shunter: 12034/53

Total
Steam: 74
Diesel: 47

On the way and including the four depots and one works that I managed to bunk, I saw a grand total of 337 mixed locomotives. Take into consideration the locos on Burton and Saltley that I saw but couldn't actually see all the numbers, it could easily have touched the 400 mark.

Today, it's Saturday and we are just turning down Station Road West. My wife pulled up outside the station as darkness descended on us. Ashleigh was asleep on the back seat, unusual for her as she's usually wide awake and raring to go with me. Not today, however. Once out of the car, I heard the announcer announcing the departure of a King's Cross train. I just caught a glimpse of it leaving the station. A single unit stood patiently awaiting departure from platform 4. A little uncanny, would you say?

I follow the same procedure that I did almost 37 years ago. My shed directory in hand and once again, child-like, I ran from the station entrance, turning sharp left and entering the brightly-lit subway. I turned another sharp left and passed the Railway Sports & Social Club which was situated on my immediate left. To my right, I noticed a small, well kept bowling green. In the distance I could see a haulage company with a fine assortment of wagons in the yard. Grimar was the name of the company. Yes, I know what you're thinking - they don't come any grimar than that.

My eyes slowly turned towards the area I wanted to see. The coal hopper, engines and the shed with its oddly designed criss-cross locomotive turning arrangements had gone. A rather large looking horse was peacefully chewing on the grass of this now baron wasteland. A very thin wire fence kept us apart but on approaching, the horse did have the courtesy to stop eating and look at me.

We stood there staring at each other. I'm bloody sure he wanted to speak, if only to tell me when and where it all went. A smile came across my face as I made my way back to the car. A small football pitch lay in silence as I walked past it, no doubt it was associated with the railway club.

I stood outside the club for a minute and I'm sure I heard people inside talking about a million and one railway stories. How many tales were told over a pint or two once the day's work was over and the families and friends of those great, great workmates of yesteryear were gathered for an evening out together?

Once inside the car, my wife handed me a sandwich followed by a nice piping hot cup of coffee. I sat there for a while but I felt compelled to take just one more look around the station area. Steamers buffet looked very inviting, a quiet place for a drink or a sandwich before your train arrived. The station itself looked spotless and you could sense that old fashioned word "pride" was in everything I viewed. The same pride that the old railway folk had all those years ago. The lady station announcer announced a non-stop service to King's Cross approaching and she advised one and all to "stand well away from the platform edge!" It flashed through and as it passed the 115mph board my hand tried in desperation to touch it. To touch the past.

Ashleigh was still asleep as we departed. I noticed the shop lights going out as we turned away from a nearby shopping centre set in this lovely little area. The long journey home was spent chatting to my wife about future trips out into the partially unknown. Ashleigh very kindly joined in the conversation as we travelled through the outskirts of Nottingham.

"Where we orf to next Dad?," she enquired.

"Oh, let's wait and see," I answered.

"Sheffield was mentioned before Christmas," she said.

"We'll see, babe. We'll just have to wait and see," I said.

We arrived home after 6pm. The shopping put away and now time for our tea. Tea over and done with it's time for me to go orf to work. I'll finish this story on Monday afternoon, because it's a bit difficult to do with tears in my eyes.

Locomotives on Grantham shed, 34F, 31st January, 1963

Steam

Class 4 2-6-0: 43087/111/59
A3 4-6-2: 60042/9/54/6/63/105/6/11
V2 2-6-2: 60814/905/6
B1 4-6-0: 61251/367/89/92
O2 2-8-0: 63923/8/30/1/2/5/40/2/8/9/56/63/8/73/4/81/4/7
WD 2-8-0: 90025/598/696

Diesel

Brush Type 4: D1511
BR 350hp 0-6-0 shunter: D3445/87
English Electric 'Deltic' Type 5: D9013/4

Total

Steam: 39
Diesel: 5

"SORRY LAD, YOU'RE A WEEK TOO LATE!"

I had chosen the right day for another trip into the halcyon days of steam and diesel traction. Oh, and shed bunking.

Monday 21st February, 2000 was a fantastic day weatherwise. Ashleigh and I were up very early and were purchasing our tickets from Duddeston station to Llandudno Junction at 07.55. The adult fare for a Day Return was £15.25, child £2. We boarded a local service into New Street, then the 08.10 service to our destination.

As we brushed past Basford Hall we could see the usual sad sight of dead and derelict diesels scattered around this one-time great steam stronghold. On the far side of Crewe station we could see another row of diesels awaiting their fate.

A nice little surprise awaited us as we departed the station. Apart from a handful of diesels including D6502, D6529, D6553, D2073, D8233 and D1842 there were two steam locomotives standing side by side in the Crewe Heritage Centre. A Standard 2-6-4T, No. 80063, and, being attended by two locomen, Standard class 7P6F No. 70000 *Britannia*.

Passing the electric depot I saw several different classes but they were partially hidden from view. However, I managed to see and note 92017.

We arrived in Chester and once again, like so many stations we have visited, it had the air of yesterday about it - apart from the new Alstom diesel unit depot, which looked totally out of place surrounded by the echoes of yesterday's busy railways.

We finally arrived at Llandudno Junction. The class 37 that had hauled us was No. 37421. These locomotives and their stock are going to be replaced after the winter timetable expires.

We followed the shed directory partially towards the old steam depot that was coded 6G on the only ever visit I made, whilst on holiday - on Monday 27th July, 1964. The six-road straight shed was of LNWR origin and it had been demolished week commencing 14th February, 2000. It had closed to steam sometime in 1966; all that remained now was the old amenity block. In the station, awaiting departure to Holyhead, was an original green DMU. It still had the British Railways insignia on its sides.

Talking of DMUs, a service was announced over the p.a. system and a two-car set stood on platform one. I must be honest and admit I never really took any notice of the announcement. However, I should have done. The reason being, we were planning to return to Rhyl on the first available service because my daughter wanted to spend some time in the amusement arcades. That was the plan, but standing in the platform as I've said, was a two-car set. I thought it was our train back to Rhyl because it was nearly

10.41 when we boarded. The train departed with Ashleigh and me on board. We bounced out of the station and, on our arrival at Tal-y-Cafn, we were notified by the guard that we were heading towards Blaenau Ffestiniog. Now, I've never been to Blaenau Ffestiniog and I certainly didn't want to go, either. Once we were well away from the station I asked my daughter to walk a few yards away whilst I cursed my luck. The return service to Llandudno was not until 12.32. And there was no way that I was going to sit and wait for it.

We began walking the seven bloody miles to Llandudno Junction but a passing motorist stopped and within ten minutes we were back at the Junction. The good Lord really does love me - he just likes a bit of fun now and then. We boarded the next train to Chester and this time we, I, got it right.

"Yippee!," my daughter said as she boarded the train.

On our arrival in Chester, we quickly set about walking to the old depot that M. and D. and I bunked way back on a miserable wet and cold Sunday 10th March, 1963. Chester (Midland) was an LNWR shed and it closed in 1967. However, it was full of steam engines on the day we visited and there was a good mixture on, 40 to be exact plus a single diesel shunter, D2388.

Today, part of the Green Lane housing estate stands on the site of the steam shed. The estate, like the shed area, overlooks the main Chester-Crewe lines. I remember standing there watching a Black Five hauling a passenger service in from Crewe. The black smoke roared out of its chimney as it thundered out of the old station. Silly, but I stood there waving at the passengers seated in their compartments. Some actually waved back.

Ashleigh and I scampered back to the station and on our arrival I asked a couple of railwaymen about the other depot out at 6B, Mold Junction. I was given conflicting information so I thought if we go there and there's nothing to see it will have been a complete waste of time. If we don't go there I'll never really know what's there, if anything. I decided to catch the local service to Shotton.

The old shed was situated close to Saltney Ferry station. It was an eight-road straight shed and on Sunday 10th March, 1963 David, Melvin and I bunked it. There were 25 steam locos on, including No. 1002 *County of Buckinghamshire*, also a Western Region 2-8-0, No. 2890. Another Western loco stood inside the shed, No. 6997 *Bryn-Ivor Hall*, also a single diesel shunter in the shape of 12053.

As the train flashed past the old shed it was, as one of the railway staff pointed out to me, still standing but it was a scrap metal company now. On our arrival at Shotton, class 66 No. 66008 ran overhead on a steel train.

Locomotives on Mold Junction shed, 6B, 10th January, 1963

Steam

GWR County 4-6-0: 1002
GWR 28xx 2-8-0: 2890
GWR Hall 4-6-0: 6997
LMS 4F 0-6-0: 44359
LMS Class 5 2-6-0: 42885/933
LMS Class 5 4-6-0: 44874/917/5001/39/197/348/438
LMS 3F 0-6-0T: 47350/410/627/46/73
LMS 8F 2-8-0: 48356/555/667
BR Class 5 4-6-0: 73126
WD 2-8-0: 90291/503/709

Diesel

LMS 350hp 0-6-0 shunter: 12053

Total Steam: 25 Diesel: 1

Once on board our return service to Chester I asked the guard for his permission to take a photo of the shed from his open cab window. He stood there looking at me, no doubt he thought I was joking but once I'd produced my camera he smiled and escorted me into his cab. On passing the shed I managed to take three photos in quick succession. I hope they all turn out.

On our arrival at Chester, we joined the Birmingham via Shrewsbury service, alighting at Wrexham General where Ashleigh took charge of the Locoshed Directory and led us to another depot that the three of us bunked on the same day in 1963. Once we had crossed the level crossing we found a small metal gate barring our entrance. However, we soon climbed over that and made our way towards where the old enclosed roundhouse once stood.

The shed was coded 89B on the day we visited. It had just 36 steam locos on, on that day 37 years ago. Today, just wasteland awaited us. The yard that once stood on the opposite side of the main line is now a housing estate. Actually, it's called Llys David Lloyd George Estate.

On our way out we passed the signal box and I had a chat with one

Locomotives on Croes Newydd shed, 89B, 10th March, 1963

GWR 16xx 0-6-0PT: 1628/32/60
GWR 57xx 0-6-0PT: 3630/749/4683/5774/9608/9790
GWR 28XX 2-8-0: 3815
GWR 43xx 2-6-0: 5399/6301/39
GWR 56xx 0-6-2T: 5679/6604/10/1/7/32/74/94/8
GWR 74xx 0-6-0PT: 7414/8/31/43
LMS Class 2 2-6-0: 46507
BR 8F 2-8-0: 48260/330/757
BR Class 4 4-6-0: 75006/20/7/9
BR Class 4 2-6-4T: 80079/80

Total: 36 steam. No diesels.

Graham Priddon. He had just finished his shift and was heading off home when I managed to have a word with him about Oswestry.

We chatted for a while, mostly about railways, but he did say that the branch line to Oswestry had gone, so had the station building and, as for the shed and small adjoining workshops, he knew very little except that they were no longer there. He said he would make some enquiries for me and send any information to me by letter. I thanked him and we made our way back to Wrexham General station.

We sat on an old bench in the sunshine and ate our lunch. I felt rather sad about the passing into history of so many sheds and yards. But in all honesty I knew what to expect on our travels and it was just the moment that upset me.

We boarded another local service to Chester, then it was time to say goodbye, and head off towards Crewe. On our arrival, I managed to get all the loco numbers in and around the station and shed area before we headed towards Stoke.

We arrived in darkness and I was advised that the old straight shed was a cash and carry. The chap that I spoke to had no idea what stood on the site of the old roundhouse. We boarded our final train home and arrived indoors a little after 8.30pm. The weather had been very kind to us and it had been a very mixed but emotional and enjoyable day, just like it was all those years ago with my old school chums, M. and D.

My nan came from Burslem in Staffordshire. She was born in 1900. On several occasions, I visited her relatives and friends when I was just a little lad. I remember we walked up many a steep hill and I recall we laughed as we scampered back down the hills as we made our way to the railway station. The train ride home to New Street was great fun for a youngster.

In later life, I would come to this area for another reason - train spotting. I visited this depot on a couple of occasions, one of them being on Sunday 17th January, 1965. I bunked the straight shed and the roundhouse which had a total of 68 mixed locos on. It was rumoured that the shed foreman instructed the enginemen to point the steam locos facing outward in the roundhouse. This was to make it difficult for the spotters to get the loco numbers. It may have been a ploy to make it more time-consuming but if they had hung these engines upside down I would still have got them and it would not have delayed me, I can tell you that. Nothing was allowed to delay or train spotting trips. The bad winter of 1962/3 never stopped us, so a few engines placed awkwardly certainly wouldn't.

It's strange, but true. We never gave the bunking of any sheds, yards or workshops a thought. I can't recall ever sitting down with Melvin or David and discussing the trip we were about to embark on. Melvin simply stated

Locomotives on Stoke shed, 5D, 17th January, 1965

LMS Fairburn Class 4 2-6-4T: 42066/69/70/160/209/24/97
LMS Stanier Class 4 2-6-4T: 42474/85/542/64/90/609/63/9
LMS Class 4 2-6-0: 43022/52/118
Midland Rly 3F 0-6-0: 43605
LMS 4F 0-6-0: 44079/344/421/32/96
LMS Class 5 4-6-0: 44713/852/950/5074/89/93/191/240/387/440
LMS 3F 0-6-0T: 47273/80/587/96/649/64
LMS 8F 2-8-0: 48018/56/90/2/131/47/62/246/8/55/70/388/446/52/548/51/5/736
BR Class 5 4-6-0: 73015
BR Class 4 4-6-0: 75018/31/40/56
BR Class 4 2-6-0: 76020/44/51/75
BR Class 2 2-6-0: 78017

Total Steam: 68   No diesels

we were going here or there on this day or that, usually a Sunday, although Tamworth was regularly visited on Saturdays during the summer months. We also visited the local sheds during the light nights and on no occasion was a depot ever discussed, apart from how we would go about bunking it.

It's funny when I look back at some of the things we got up to. Melvin talked his way into a dozen or so depots that at the time were a little difficult to do. However, he got the three of us in and we stuck together for almost four years. That's a lifetime to some people. Odd, really, in all the time we spent in each other's company and on a hundred trips or more, we never argued or fell out over anything, such a friendship.

DOWN THE DIP INTO SHEFFIELD MIDLAND

On Sunday 3rd March, 1963 I, along with M. and D. met up at our usual spot near the booking office window at Birmingham New Street station. The time was around 10.30am and the train to Sheffield via Derby departed at 10.50. It left from platform 7 and I recall it was a through service from Bristol to Leeds. The fare, I believe, was about 7/6 in old money.

We wrote down all the locos that were visible on Saltley shed as we hurried past it. The next depots along the way were at Burton, Derby, Hasland and finally, Millhouses. This was the last depot before Sheffield Midland. On arrival via the single line that ran and dipped into the station, our first priority was to hurry out of the station and board the bus for 41A Darnall.

I honestly can't remember if it was a number 71 Elm Tree bus or a number 52 Ballifield or Handsworth bus we boarded out to the depot. But we arrived to find the old GCR shed packed. With no time to spare, we bunked the 10-road straight shed and scurried out within 10 minutes of our arrival. There were 38 mixed steam locos on plus 47 mixed diesels, including D0280 *Falcon*.

Locomotives on Sheffield Darnall, 41A, 3rd March, 1963

Steam

LMS Patriot 4-6-0: 45536
LMS Jubilee 4-6-0: 45570/94/656
LMS 8F 2-8-0: 48200
LNER B1 4-6-0: 61044/50/1/94/109/43/52/210/49/72/305/13/5/72/7
GCR O4 2-8-0: 63574/609/21/4/45/58/95/737/42/64/83/821/2/81/902
LNER O1 2-8-0: 63856
WD 2-8-0: 90162/582

Diesel

Brush Type 4 prototype: D0280
BR 350hp 0-6-0 shunter: D3131/702/4050/1/65/74/82/5/90/4
Brush Type 2: D5520/684/99/805/11/3/23/5/6/38/44/5/51
English Electric Type 3: D6745/6/7/8/9/50/4/96/802/3/6/8/10/1/2/4/58
English Electric Type 1: D8023/53/4/60/1/3

Total Steam: 38 Diesel: 47

The next depot on our list was over at 41B Grimesthorpe. On arrival we quickly bunked the roundhouse and we logged a mixture of 38 diesel locos. Not bad when you consider it closed in 1961. For some unknown reason, I never recorded the fact that we made our way over to 41D Canklow. I remember we caught several buses to get us there and I distinctly remember eating our snap on passing Rotherham Central station.

On returning to Sheffield Midland station we boarded a Chesterfield service and bunked both sheds in the area. Firstly, 41E Staveley Barrow Hill then another bus ride over to 41H Staveley(GC.) We noted 40 steam locos and two diesels on 41E. There were 37 steam locos and six diesels on 41H. I copped three and 20 respectively. Overall, I copped 119 mixed locos that day.

The lads and I only made one visit to Tinsley and that was on an unforgettable and very miserable wet Sunday 3rd January, 1965. We bunked the shed and the fuelling point cautiously. It was a first for us and we noticed workmen everywhere. On reflection, I think we were lucky to bunk this one. I recall we sat on the bus for over half an hour just to get to this shed out in the sticks. Then we had another tedious journey back to the station.

We visited the Chesterfield and Sheffield area on several occasions. We also visited Doncaster via Mexborough. The shed out at 36E Retford GNR was also visited and bunked in those halcyon days of steam. I must admit I always looked forward to our trips in this very busy area with its mixture of steel, coal and mineral traffic that was once the pride of this great city of a thousand and one hills.

But that was yesterday and sadly those days belong to yesterday. So, let's cheer ourselves up and take a look at what's there now. Today it's Saturday 19th February, 2000. Once again my wife Carol and my daughter Ashleigh are going to keep me company as we travel down Memory Lane. It's a bloody cold, wet morning as we are just putting our lunch into the car. The tank's full of petrol, everyone's ready so let's hit the road Jack and see what's in store for us today.

The time is just approaching 10.56 and we've hit a problem. My wife has changed her mind because she doesn't feel too good all of a sudden. I'll hang on a while just in case it's only a passing tummy upset. It's just coming up to 12 o'clock and the trip is definitely off. I'll take another look at it another time.

Monday morning, 28th February, 2000. Ashleigh and I are going to Doncaster and we hope to revisit all the sheds in that area. The first depot will be Derby. Oh no it won't. Ashleigh doesn't feel very well, so the trip's cancelled.

Saturday morning 4th March, 2000. We are finally pulling out of the drive and heading towards Sheffield via the motorway. Hip hip hooray! The first shed on our itinery was 41A Darnall. The usual concrete and glass awaited us as we pulled up outside the station at 12.15. The overhead electrification had long gone, so had the locomotives that were once housed at this shed. Today, the only sound I heard was the whistling of the wind over   barren land.

By the year 2000 this was all that remained of the once big diesel depot at Tinsley, opened in the mid-1960s, closed just 30 years later. *(Alex Scott)*

The diesel depot over at Tinsley was our next port of call. We arrived at 12.35. I stood on the bridge and stared down at the one-time busy marshalling yard with its hump yard and fuelling point. The locos and wagons that once upon a time came and went are just memories to me. I could clearly see three dead class 08 shunters. A single class 60 stood attached to a rake of loaded bogie bolster wagons. The shed itself that until quite recently housed a grand variety of diesel locos was gone, except for a small building. I couldn't make out exactly what it was.

We sat in the car and ate our lunch before moving on to our third shed of the day. My wife was driving as usual and she followed the route according to the advice I gave her from my faithful old shed directory. However, we missed our turning into White Hall Road where the old shed was once situated. We found ourselves parked in the village of Canklow. The time was 1pm.

At precisely two minutes past one we were surrounded by armed police. An officer in a police car indicated to us by hand signal to reverse our car and get out of the area straight away. My wife hadn't changed gear when we could see a police helicopter hovering overhead. Within seconds I could see several police cars flying in all directions. We drove slowly and as we passed another police car the road was being cordoned off. The helicopter was still hovering above us.

Once we were clear of the area and driving very slowly down the Bawtry Road, I pointed out to my wife and daughter that the police had surrounded what looked like some houses that stood adjacent to some boarded up shops. We could only hazard a guess as to what happened, but the sight of armed police gave us some indication that it was definitely a siege.

My wife put the radio on but there was nothing on except music being played and local radio advertising. At 13.25 we arrived in White Hall Road. I followed the directory and it led me to a housing estate. Carol parked the car on the car park of The Sidings public house. That was clue enough for me that the estate may just be called The Sidings Estate. Once inside the pub, I enquired about the old steam shed. I described it to several locals. It was coded 41D in 1959, a Midland roundhouse which sadly closed its doors some time in 1965. The couple I spoke to agreed with each other that the housing estate which the locals referred to as The Sidings Estate was in fact built on the site of the former Eastern Region shed. I thanked them and departed.

The helicopter was still hovering when we left Canklow at 13.45. The short drive to Doncaster had us all chatting about the events that had taken place. We were very excited at what had happened to us and all because we took a wrong turning. It was a classic case of being in the wrong place at the right time, adventure-wise that is.

We arrived outside the main entrance to 36A Doncaster at 14.05. I donned my high-visibility vest and entered through the main doors. I approached the depot foreman and as I tried to explain who I was and what I was doing there, he just said: "Come in, there's all the numbers on the board. Help yourself, I'm busy."

"Of course," I thought to myself. "They're relieving each other at 14.00." I quickly wrote down the list of locos on shed, thanked the gaffer and departed hastily.

I made my way back to the car and once inside I asked Carol to pull away slowly and head for the rear of the shed. I pointed her in the right direction. I could see all the engines that were stabled there and I took two photos. The area was as it was years ago, massive. The 13-road shed had been pulled down some time in the '80s or '90s according to those I spoke to. The four-road small maintenance depot still stood apart from the original building.

The actual shed was a straight shed of Great Northern origin, closed to steam in 1966. The locomotives that were allocated to the depot were A3s, A1s, V2s, B1s, and O2 2-8-0s. The coal hopper stood to the left of the shed looking north. The 70ft turntable was especially built to turn the A4s and this was situated towards the station looking north. I was told a very interesting little story by a driver who wishes to remain anonymous: "Those who worked at the depot during the Fifties and Sixties and were of UK origin washed in the ablutions, whilst those who were not from the UK washed in the old tin buckets."

We drove into the town centre, parked the car up, Alex put his hand into his pockets and we were all treated to a MacDonalds and milk shakes. We spent a short time in the station area and thoughts of Melvin and David came to mind.

The works looked so forlorn, a handful of wagons stood patiently awaiting their turn to go into the old works and hopefully be returned to their former glory.

Sadly, the steam engines that Melvin, David and I saw that summer Sunday in 1962 will never return. We bunked the works and shed on that super, nerve-racking day. We noted in the works and on the shed over 200 locomotives. Today at the station, local services to Sheffield and Scunthorpe were announced. They came and went in between the arrival and departure

Locomotives on Doncaster shed, 36A, 22nd July, 1962

Steam

Class 4 2-6-4T: 42038
A4 4-6-2: 60024
A3 4-6-2: 60036/85
A1/1 4-6-2: 60113
A1 4-6-2: 60122/39/49
A2 4-6-2: 60500/20/3
V2 2-6-2: 60828/72/902/5/23/4/36/66
B1 4-6-0: 61001/36/55/87/93/122/4/7/36/51/7/8/86/96/233/50/5/79/326
K3 2-6-0: 61812/25
K1 2-6-0: 62036/66/9/81
O4 2-8-0: 63593/607/13/8/92/3/8/702/802/58/84
O1 2-8-0: 63678
O2 2-8-0: 63922/6/7/56/63/5/76/7/84
J50 0-6-0T: 68917/28/71/2/6
Britannia 4-6-2: 70010
Class 2 2-6-0: 78022/5
WD 2-8-0: 90001/3/53/63/144/50/80/224/35/55/86/305/442/56/76/80/94/501/22/51/9/
 90569/627/36/62/83
9F 2-10-0: 92039/137/9/68/70/2/86/90/1/2

Diesel

Sulzer Type 4 'Peak': D96
English Electric Type 4: D348/51/97
BR 350hp 0-6-0 shunter: D3483/4079/12125
Birmingham RC&W Type 2: D5347/404/5
Brush Type 2: D5550/692
English Electric Type 3: D6769
English Electric Type 5 'Deltic': D9003/7/15/21

Total
Steam: 109
Diesel: 17

of a Glasgow express and two services to King's Cross, hauled by class 91s. A class 37 arrived light engine, stopped, then headed to the shed.

It was time to say a fond farewell to Doncaster. The weather had once again been very kind to us. We sat in the car talking about our day so far, and we smiled as my wife said: "I wonder if that helicopter's still hovering overhead in the pleasant mining village of Canklow?"

Our car engine revved up and we departed sunny Doncaster. I know that Ashleigh and I will be back here soon, because we still have to visit Retford via yesterday's memories of Doncaster.

Locomotives in Doncaster Works, 22nd July, 1962

Steam

LMS Class 5 4-6-0: 44805
Jubilee 4-6-0: 45712
3F 0-6-0T: 47534
8F 2-8-0: 48060
A4 4-6-2: 60009/30
A3 4-6-2: 60039/49/63/5/7/100
A1 4-6-2: 60125
A2 4-6-2: 60527/32
B1 4-6-0: 61027/83/150/1/5
J11 0-6-0: 64406/42
Britannia 4-6-2: 70000/2/36
BR Class 5 4-6-0: 73135
WD 2-8-0: 90042/508

Total

Steam: 28
Diesel: 31

Diesels noted around the Works area and the station

Sulzer Type 4 'Peak': D20/62/74/82/91/7/112/7/24/5/41/57/62
English Electric Type 4: D285
BR 350hp 0-6-0 shunter: D3482/659/85/97/703/845/4042/55/62/70/81/2/94
Brush Type 2: D5836/8/9
English Electric Type 5 'Deltic': D9005

A BEVY OF BEAUTIES IN BRISTOL AND BATH

It was a bitter cold Sunday morning on 11th November, 1962. The three of us stood stamping our feet trying to get some feeling back into them. The bad winter of 1962/63 had already taken its toll weather-wise and it held the country in a vice-like grip. Eventually our direct service from Birmingham New Street to Bristol via Worcester was announced. Boy oh boy were we both pleased and excited to hear and finally see our train approaching platform eight with a mixture of black and white smoke spiralling skywards out of the engine's chimney.

We had taken the unusual procedure of coming into town early because the roads and streets were treacherous. I felt that this was the main reason why we were so bloody cold. I recall my teeth chattering as I tried to make conversation with both Melvin and David. They both wore brightly knitted scarves which partially covered their mouths. They were too cold to speak.

The engine that hauled the dirty, filthy snow-covered coaches into the station was No. 45040, a Black Five. We scrambled into the first available compartment, shutting the door tightly behind us. The hissing from the pipes that ran underneath the seats was a welcome sound. The small cross-shaped knob indicated that the heaters were on "Full."

The hoot from the locomotive whistle rang out loudly and within a few seconds we were pulling out of the station. The giant engine stirred and then spluttered its way into Bath Row tunnel. Black and white smoke engulfed the train as we passed through several tunnels before we finally emerged out of the last tunnel into an eerie stillness of that grey, dark and very dull day. Everywhere you looked it was so picturesque and one could have been forgiven for thinking that he was in some sort of magical, dreamy far away place.

The train rattled its way through a handful of stations before descending the Lickey Bank to Bromsgrove. We had the windows wide open as we flew past the old loco and the banking sidings. We were lucky and noted a few. The banking locos were resting prior to another heavy train requiring their assistance up the 1 in 37 incline.

Once again, the windows were closed to shut out the cold as soon as we cleared the Bromsgrove area. Worcester locomotive depot would be the first port of call. The windows were once again wide open as we wrote down what engine numbers we could see on passing the two sheds on our right.

On arrival, we nipped off smartish in the hope of getting the locomotive numbers that were busying themselves in the yard, but they were hidden behind a hundred and one wagons.

The coldness hit our faces as we wrote down the numbers that we could see as we passed the two depots at Gloucester. The station was deadly quiet and there was nothing to note.

On arriving in Bristol our first act was to scurry off and bunk shed 82A, Bristol Bath Road. We were highly delighted with the locos on shed, but we were over the moon on seeing a Modified Hall simmering in the yard. The locomotive, I remember, was 6972 *Beningbrough Hall*. I remember the entire area was covered in snow and it crackled under our feet as we tip-toed out of the area.

The next depot we bunked was over the bridge at 82B, St. Phillips Marsh. There were 56 on. Finally, 82E Barrow Road was duly bunked - a superb shed as you can see from the cover of Fearless Ghosts.

A short train ride to Bath and after a 20-minute walk, trot and falling arse-over-head twice we all arrived slightly bruised at 82F, Bath Green Park.

The old shed at Bristol Bath Road goes way back to the early days of steam. It became a 10-road straight shed after a rebuilding programme by the GWR in the 1930s. The original depot had two roundhouses. The turntable was adjacent to a small workshop. It closed to steam in 1960. In the years that followed, a small three-road fuel point was positioned just a

Locomotives on Bristol Barrow Road shed, 82E, 11th November, 1962

Steam

GWR 2251 0-6-0: 2229
GWR 57xx 0-6-0PT: 3606/32/75/7/96/702/52/65/95/4619/8725/95/9615/23/6
GWR 5101 2-6-2T: 4131
GWR 52xx 2-8-0T: 5203/15
GWR 61xx 2-6-2T: 6147
LMS Class 2 2-6-2T: 41207/8/48/9
Midland Rly 3F 0-6-0: 43245
Midland Rly 4F 0-6-0: 43924
LMS 4F 0-6-0: 44092/135/208/11/64/9/466/520/3/34/55/69
LMS Class 5 4-6-0: 44663/839/41/53/947/5186
LMS Jubilee 4-6-0: 45562/73/690
LMS Class 2 2-6-0: 46506
LMS 8F 2-8-0: 48101/212
L&YR 0F 0-4-0ST: 51218
BR Class 5 4-6-0: 73015/28/92/6
BR Class 4 4-6-0: 75071/2
BR Class 3 2-6-2T: 82007/36/7/9/40/3
BR 9F 2-10-0: 92004/7/2221/48
BR Crosti 9F 2-10-0: 92029

Diesel

BR 204hp 0-6-0 shunter: D2134/5/45
BR 350hp 0-6-0 shunter: D3803

Total Steam: 68 Diesel: 4

few yards away from the shed signal box. Another small yard lay close to the workshop and was visible from the station area if you looked westwards.

St. Phillips Marsh was a good 15 minutes walk from Temple Meads station but only a short five-minute walk if you followed the railway bridge route which we did. It was tucked away behind Bath Road shed. During the late 1950s and early '60s it had over 60 0-6-0 pannier tanks plus Halls and Granges. This old roundhouse closed to steam in 1964.

Bristol Barrow Road closed in 1965. It was a former Midland Railway shed and a roundhouse by design. However, the Western Region took it over from the London Midland Region in 1958. GWR locomotives eventually replaced the LMS types. I only bunked this shed on one occasion. An interesting note of observation was that Patriot and Jubilee class locos were coaled and watered here and they often worked Bristol-Leeds services and vice-versa, Leeds Holbeck being the returning depot.

Bath Green Park was situated a good 20 minutes walk from the Spa station, however, a brisk 10-minute walk from Bath Green Park station and you were in the vicinity of the shed. The shed was the main depot for the Somerset and Dorset Railway and Green Park was the main station. Sadly, like its sister sheds, the small four-road straight shed closed with the whole line in 1966. It once housed Standards, tanks, Consul 8Fs and several 7Fs.

Locomotives on Bath Green Park shed, 82F, 11th November, 1962

Steam

GWR 57xx 0-6-0PT: 3742
LMS 4F 0-6-0: 44111/46
LMS 3F 0-6-0T: 47316/552
LMS 8F 2-8-0: 48468/660/737
LMS 7F 2-8-0: 53806/7/8/9/10
BR Class 5 4-6-0: 73051/2/4
BR Class 4 2-6-0: 76019/25
BR Class 3 2-6-2T: 82004/41   *Total* Steam: 20   No diesels

Bath Road closed some time in the mid-1990s but the main shed still stands with roads 1 - 6. The three-road fuelling depot still stands, also the three-road heavy maintenance shop. The amenity block is still there and, like the other buildings, awaits its fate. The turntable was removed and taken to Kidderminster for the Severn Valley Railway. The old loco signal box still looks impressive although decay has now set in and it's only a matter of time. "High Noon."

At nearby St. Phillips Marsh I found a rather large wholesale fruit and veg market sitting on the site of the former locomotive depot. It was built

Bristol Bath Road depot, deserted and forlorn on 17th March, 2000, the clock stopped at 11.55, the moment of total closure when the last person out turned off the electric. Originally two roundhouses, it was rebuilt by the GWR in the 1930s and became a diesel depot on 12th September, 1960. (*Alex Scott*)

either late Sixties or early Seventies. The massive railway bridge that led from the shed to the coal sidings had been removed around the same time. I noted two class 08s in the sidings, 08483 and 08822. Patiently awaiting their next turn of duty on the Bristol-Paddington-Penzance sleepers were two class 47s, 47813 and 47816. The rear HST power car from the Paddington disaster was inside the newly-built maintenance depot.

A large bulk transfer refuse company occupies part of the old Barrow Road shed area. The spinal road which leads towards the M32 occupies the other part. The road sign has also disappeared. My thanks to Mr. Brian Rogers, the last Barrow Road steam driver.

The do-it-yourself firm Homebase occupies most of the area where Bath Green Park shed once stood. Sainsburys is also in the vicinity. The station still stands and there are several small shops situated within its complex.

ANOTHER MAGICAL DAY!

On Sunday morning, 16th December, 1962 I, along with Melvin and David, sat as close as possible to a roaring coal fire in the waiting room on platform 5 of Snow Hill station. Suddenly, our train to Shrewsbury was announced. We looked at each other, each waiting for one of the others to be brave and be the first to venture out of the warm room and into the coldness of that wintry day.

I walked towards the door and was quickly followed by my friends. Once outside, we scampered into the nearest compartment, shutting the door tightly behind us.

"Time for some scoff, I reckon," David announced. Melvin and I nodded in

Locomotives on Shrewsbury shed, 89A, 16th December, 1962

Steam

GWR County 4-6-0: 1009/16/17/25/6
GWR 2251 0-6-0: 3205
GWR 5101 2-6-2T: 4114
GWR 57xx 0-6-0PT: 3709/4617/23/9657
GWR Hall 4-6-0: 4914/43/6/6916/7910
GWR Castle 4-6-0: 5022/43
GWR Grange 4-6-0: 6817/25/33/5/40/8/76/7
GWR 43xx 2-6-0: 6370/5/7329/36
GWR 74xx 0-6-0PT: 7442
GWR Manor 4-6-0: 7812
GWR 94xx 0-6-0PT: 9411/63/98
LMS Class 2 2-6-2T: 41203
LMS Class 5 4-6-0: 44687/858/5143
LMS Jubilee 4-6-0: 45660/90/9
LMS 8F 2-8-0: 48400/738/9
BR Class 5 4-6-0: 73026/90/5/7
BR Class 4 4-6-0: 75005
BR Class 4 2-6-4T: 80078/97/100/1/35

Diesel

BR Type 4 Warship: D831
BR 350hp 0-6-0 shunter: D3111/93

Total Steam: 55 Diesel: 3

agreement. We sat quietly munching away on our sandwiches.

"Egg again, Alex," David said, smiling to himself.

"Yes," I answered cheerfully.

I noticed Melvin had is mouth full which rendered him unable to speak. David also noticed this and began asking Melvin questions just so he could tease him.

"Ermm, what time do we arrive in Shrewsbury, Melvin? Have you ever been to Oswestry before? What's the shed like? The works, are they massive like Crewe or small like Wolverhampton?"

Melvin never answered David. He just munched away on his snap. David once again played on the fact that poor old Melvin couldn't speak because his mouth was full. He asked: "Have you lost your tongue Melvin?"

Melvin knew from his past experiences with us that David was just playing him up. But he never took any notice, just munched away on his double thick Spam sarny.

On reaching Wolverhampton Low Level, we opened the carriage window and took a peep outside on the off-chance that a loco might be knocking about. But there was nothing to see until we passed Stafford Road and Oxley sheds. After the two depots we checked our pads to see if we had copped any. Meanwhile, the train shuffled on to our next port of call, Shrewsbury.

Once the train had come to a stand we were off and scurrying towards our first shed of the day, 89A Shrewsbury. We bunked the roundhouse first, which was a GWR design. Then the two straight sheds. These were eight and nine-road sheds of LNWR origin. On that particular day we noted 68 mixed steam locomotives and three diesels, two of which were shunters, the other being a Warship, No. D831. The shed closed in 1967.

We slipped and slid our way back to the station and on arrival we soon boarded the first service to Gobowen. There we clambered into a single coach that was going to be hauled by engine No. 1432, an 0-4-2 tank. I took a photograph before we departed but unfortunately it never turned out. The scenic route was marvellous. The entire countryside was silhouetted against rolling hills and covered in pure white snow.

The old Cambrian Railway station at Oswestry was very quiet. We made our way through the slush-covered streets to the six-road straight shed. There was only 27 on and I copped 26. The depot closed on 18th January, 1965. The works looked very impressive and we anticipated a few in there but we were to be disappointed. There was only four inside the workshops. I copped three. A quick return to the station and once again we boarded our single coach back to Gobowen. Then on to Shrewsbury and the first train back to Snow Hill. On arrival we bade each other our usual goodnight and "see you in school tomorrow."

Today it's Saturday 8th April, 2000 and I'm being joined by my wife for another day out. This time we're off to Oswestry. The weather is totally different from that winter's day 37 years ago, in fact it's a very hot day and we're skimpily dressed. We enjoyed the pleasant journey and arrived just around lunchtime at the site of the former steam depot.

Today, the Richard Burbridge Decorative Timber Wholesale Warehouse occupies the site just a few yards from Whittington Road. He also has another large building on the other side of Unicorn Road. The works that we bunked in '62 still stands, but it now belongs to another firm, Cambrian House Antiques.

The station entrance still stands, but it's boarded up. It's called Cambrian Autoparts and it once belonged to Mr. Owen. Mr. owen owns a very lucrative coach company amongst other business interests. The other station building was demolished some years ago.

We parked the car in a small car park that was actually part of the small but very interesting Oswestry Museum. We had a short tour of the town before returning to the car park. I was very fortunate in meeting an ex-railway employee. Mr. John Humphreys very kindly escorted me around the museum. I was thrilled to death when the first thing I noticed was a Hall class engine tucked just inside the entrance, No. 5952 *Cogan Hall*

"The loco is going to be restored to its former glory and as you can see the tender is in first class condition," John explained. The engine's boiler was in need of some urgent repair work. The plates on the side of the cab were in fantastic condition. I noticed there was a fine assortment of old motorbikes on view. Also in the small museum was memorabilia by the score. I urge anyone who's interested in the history of Oswestry to visit this Aladdin's cave.

I ventured outside and came across an old Hudswell works shunter, plus two old 0-6-0 Jinties in very dilapidated condition, plus another couple of works shunters in poor condition plus some old coaching stock.

Some interesting news came from John prior to us departing for lunch: "Alex, a trust has been set up to open the line from Oswestry station to Gobowen at a cost of £250,000. The town council and the Borough Council have both pledged £5000 each as a deposit towards the cost. Then, yearly payments interest free until the debt has been fully paid up over a 10-year period." A short pause followed while he took his breath. "The line is still in place from the old steam days and it only needs a mile of track to reach Gobowen," he concluded.

I shook his hand and we parted company. I had enjoyed my brief visit to Oswestry and meeting John was a real bonus. We drove through the town and headed towards a small but informal restaurant where we had our lunch. Ashleigh has gone to Drayton Manor for the day and this is the first trip she's missed. Anyway, it's saved me a few quid on her lunch. Only joking.

THE LONGEST HAUL

Ashleigh and I were up at 4.30am on Monday 17th April, 2000. We had packed a bag each containing clothes and hopefully enough scoff for our three day jaunt around Lancashire, Cumbria, Glasgow, Edinburgh, Newcastle, Yorkshire and Leeds. Our intention was to revisit all the sheds that I visited on my own plus some that I visited with Melvin and David in the heydays of steam.

The early morning rain followed us from our front door in Birmingham all the way up the east coast to Morpeth which is situated about 15 miles north of Newcastle.

The first shed we visited was 8F, Wigan Springs Branch. It was originally a 12-road straight shed and closed to steam on 12th April, 1966. Today a locomotive component recovery and distribution centre occupies the three-road former diesel maintenance shed.

We glanced around the shed and then bunked part of the yard with caution. An assortment of locos there included 08233, 08693, 08952, 37011, 37012, 37153, 37020, 37154, 37043, 37431, 56080, 56095 and 56127. We were doing fine until we were spotted by a workman. I had Ashleigh to think about so we scurried away from the depot yard.

"Dad, they're only scrap, not to worry," Ashleigh said, trying to console me.

We boarded the first service heading towards our next port of call at Lancaster. The rain continued to follow us northwards and on arrival at the station we only had seconds to spare before we boarded the service for Barrow-in-Furness. The shed was a good 30-minute walk from the station and consisted of a 10-road straight shed. It closed to steam on 12th December, 1966. However, we spoke to a chap who kindly gave us a lift to the shed area.

He advised us that part of the shed had been burned down. The result of an engine catching fire, the shed having been partially converted to handle diesels.

Locomotives noted on Barrow shed, 12C, 28th February, 1966

Steam

Fairburn Class 4 2-6-4T: 42236
Stanier Class 4 2-6-4T: 42610
4F 0-6-0: 44086/310/1/50/94/601
Class 5 4-6-0: 45294/5383
3F 0-6-0T: 47373/667/75
Britannia 4-6-2: 70008

Diesel

Hudswell 204hp 0-6-0 shunter: D2515/6
Metrovick Type 2 Co-Bo: D5703/4/5/10/3/8

Total   Steam: 14   Diesel: 8

The British Railways Board planned to clear the site but after finding large quantities of asbestos buried underneath the soil they deferred. Apparently, the old wagon works had cut up locomotives and coaching stock but never cleared the area afterwards. On our arrival we could see the area had been completely covered with topsoil. Approaching the area, he pointed it out to us: "You see, just an empty site."

I just gazed upon it. The area looked oh so very different from that time when I visited it on 28th February, 1966. I wrote down 24 mixed locos that were on shed. Turning to him, I said: "Thankyou."

He turned the car around and we headed back towards the station. On arrival, I thanked him again and shook his hand. Ashleigh and I hurried towards the station and we boarded the Carlisle service that took us up to Workington.

On arriving at Workington, the guard was great. He let me take a quick photograph of the old 12-road straight shed. The depot had seen better days and on passing it did look very derelict and forlorn. On my last visit on 27th February, 1966, I noted 24 mixed steam and diesel locomotives on. I copped three.

The guard approached us as we neared the outskirts of Carlisle. "That's

Locomotives on Carlisle Kingmoor shed, 12A, 3rd October, 1964

Steam

LNER Fairburn Class 4 2-6-4T: 42154
LMS Class 4 2-6-0: 43000/4/11/23/8/36/45/103
Midland Rly 4F 0-6-0: 43853/981
LMS 4F 0-6-0: 44305/457
LMS Class 5 4-6-0: 44667/96/726/8/92/818/20/84/8/901/28/5013/61/75/120/6/48/67/
    45204/17/25/54/75/93/5/316/29/91/3/415/81
LMS Patriot 4-6-0: 45527/31
LMS Jubilee 4-6-0: 45574/84/8/658/742
LMS Royal Scot 4-6-0: 46128/60
LMS 3F 0-6-0T: 47671
LMS 8F 2 8 0: 48104/38/58/85/318
LNER A3 4-6-2: 60041
LNER V2 2-6-2: 60931/57
LNER B1 4-6-0: 61272
BR Britannia 4-6-2: 70006/37/40
BR Clan 4-6-2: 72005/7/8/9
BR Class 4 2-6-0: 76073
WD 2-8-0: 90706/18
BR 9F 2-10-0: 92009/10/2/5/9/52/65/130/58
BR Crosti 9F 2-10-0: 92021/6

Diesel

Sulzer Type 4 Peak: D182
Birmingham RC&W Type 2: D5310
English Electric Type 1: D8123

Total Steam: 84 Diesel: 3

the old six-road straight shed at Currock," he kindly pointed out. In the yard stood 56121, surrounded by a variety of wagons and coaching stock awaiting attention.

We had passed the one-time LNWR shed at 12B Carlisle Upperby on several occasions whilst we took a holiday in Ayrshire and other parts of Scotland some years ago. However, my last visit was in the early hours of 28th February, 1966 when I bunked this massive 32-spoke wheel design roundhouse. There were 24 on including several Brits but I copped a grand total of one, 2-6-4T No. 42094. The shed closed to steam on 12th December, 1966.

I felt it was worth taking a walk even though the rain was still falling. Ashleigh and I were soaking wet as we arrived at the depot. We took a quick look around this now partially deserted area. Within minutes we were heading back towards the station. The service to Motherwell was announced and as soon as it arrived we boarded this Glasgow-bound train. I felt a touch of sadness as I glanced out of the window when we passed the yard at Kingmoor.

The eight-road straight shed of Caledonian Railway origin had 142 steam engines allocated there in the 1950s. With the passing of time these were reduced but in 1965 there were still 119 on the books. That fact alone tells the story of just how much work there still was in this one-time fantastic area. Sadly, the shed closed on 1st January, 1968.

On my last visit I walked there in total darkness. I recall that 45-minute walk frightened me. On arrival, I bunked the shed at speed. There were just 60 on and I copped seven. Today, there's nothing visible of the old steam shed but the diesel depot on the opposite side of the main lines still stands. It closed some time in the 1980s and has recently been reopened by a private freight operator, Direct Rail Services, as a base for its class 20s and 37s. The very much slimmed down marshalling yard is still in use, two class 08s were shunting and three class 66s were knocking about at the north end.

Motherwell station was rain sodden as we pulled in. The first thing we did was to partially walk and partially trot to the shed. On arrival, we were handed on request a list of all the engines on site. This was followed by a quick unofficial tour of the shed. The first thing that struck me about this shed was that it had a rather new roof. The eight-road straight shed was an ex-Caley depot and it was rather busy as we toddled around.

On my first and last visit to this shed, I bunked it on a wintry morning of Saturday 22nd January, 1965. The shed was reasonably full with 33 on. I copped 27. The list I'd been handed contained 24, though in the yards I spotted two 08s and a class 86 but our tour didn't take us that far because safety first was the order of the day. I thanked the young driver for his time and we departed.

The service to another large shed in the area found us at Hamilton. The old 10-road straight shed had long been demolished. It closed in 1962. In '65 I noted just one Barclay 0-4-0 shunter resting inside the complex area, loco No. D2410. I copped it. Today, a housing estate and elderly people's homes stand on the site. Sainsburys supermarket was also built close to the shed.

I bunked the shed at 66A Polmadie just after dinnertime on Saturday 22nd January, 1965. The streets were covered in snow and everywhere I walked there was slush. My feet were wet and I was very cold. On that abysmal afternoon I noted 94 mixed locos in and around the ex-Caledonian 14-road straight shed. I copped 67. Sadly, all that remains of this great depot is a small maintenance area and some coaching stock awaiting attention, although there is a modern Alstom train maintenance depot on the opposite side of the main lines.

The short trip into Central station then on to 67A Corkerhill. The small six-road straight shed closed on 1st May, 1967. On that wintry day in 1965 I wrote down 34, copped 32. Today, as we worked our way cautiously around the area, I discovered that there was a new six-road straight shed dealing with several classes of DMUs and EMUs. The depot today maintains such units as class 150, 156 and 314.

We returned to Central and boarded a Dalmuir service via Yoker. On my arrival in 1965 I found the shed to have already closed but I recall some

Locomotives on Glasgow Polmadie shed, 66A, 22nd January, 1965

Steam

LMS Fairburn Class 4 2-6-4T: 42192/9/264/6/694
LMS Stanier Class 4 2-6-4T: 42613
LMS Class 5 4-6-0: 44767/5262/455
LMS 8F 2-8-0: 48524
LNER A2 4-6-2: 60512/22/24/35
BR Britannia 4-6-2: 70002/39
BR Class 5 4-6-0: 73059/60/1/2/4/72/3/6/98/103/21
BR Class 4 2-6-0: 76004/70
BR Class 4 2-6-4T: 80002/27/58/106/7/8/9/10/5/30

Diesel

Sulzer Type 4 Peak: D135
English Electric Type 4: D290/4/328
Brush Type 4: D1632
Barclay 204hp 0-4-0 shunter: D2427/8/31/2/3
BR 350hp 0-6-0 shunter: D3199/200/614/906/9/11/2/3/4/5/6/20/1
English Electric Type 1: D8056/85/115/6/8/9/23/5/6/7
Clayton Type 1: D8507/8/12/6/7/9/22/3/7/8/9/30/2/3/6/8/41/7/50

Total

Steam: 39
Diesel: 52

shunting taking place at about 5.50am. Today, Class 303 and 320 EMUs are stabled there; there are bay platforms at the Garscadden end and several sidings at the Yoker station end.

The depot at Dawsholm was also found to be closed upon my arrival in 1965. Today, the site is a housing estate. The shed at 65E Kipps was bunked and I noted 10 mixed diesel locos on the small three-road straight shed. Today the site is unused. Parkhead 65C had a real treat in store for me back in 1965. Apart from having 13 diesels in and around the six-road straight shed, it had five dead steam locomotives all in a line. I believe the first was an old Highland Railway 4-4-0 No. 54398, the next was Caledonian 4-2-2 No. 123, built in 1886. There was also locomotive No. 103, a Jones Highland Railway goods design 4-6-0 dating back to 1894, a Great North of Scotland 4-4-0 No. 49, and North British 4-4-0 No. 256. These engines, I believe, were occasionally used on railtours and they were all in immaculate condition. I took some photos but, alas, they never turned out.

Ashleigh and I pushed on to another extremely busy area, Eastfield. Fortunately for us, we were advised by several locals that the places we were about to visit were either unused or wasteland. However, we pushed on until we arrived at 65A Eastfield. I should have believed them.

The old North British shed had 14 roads and it was a straight shed. A diesel depot replaced it after it closed to steam in November, 1966.

Now, the land is barren.

The works at Cowlairs, later known as Springburn Road works was also closed, so was the shed at 65B St. Rollox. It closed its doors to steam on 7th November, 1965. On that wintry day when I visited, I noted a fine mixture of steam and diesels on site. I copped 21 out of the 32 that were there. Inside the works, I noted another 32 and copped 14.

The rain continued as we headed off to Edinburgh. The eight road straight shed at 64B Haymarket closed to steam on 9th September, 1963. However, on that Saturday evening in 1965, I noted no less than 36 mixed diesels on, copping 23. Today a diesel depot still occupies the steam shed area with seven roads looking east and eight looking west. The old coal yard has disappeared, so have the old houses that once stood nearby.

The shed at St. Margaret's was coded 64A and when I visited there were 48 on this six-road straight shed with a couple spread out in the open roundhouse. I copped 38. Today, the Meadowbank stadium occupies part of the old North British shed. Finally, over at 64C Dalry Road, I wrote down 21 locomotives in and around the old four-road straight shed that was closed on 3rd October, 1965. The shed was of Caledonian origin. Now it's part of the western approach road.

It was very late so we decided to push on to another area before we called it a day. We arrived in Morpeth later than expected because of a signal

Locomotives on Edinburgh St. Margaret's shed, 64A, 22nd January, 1965

Steam
LMS Class 5 4-6-0: 44975/5477
LMS Jubilee 4-6-0: 45715
LMS Class 2 2-6-0: 46462
LNER A3 4-6-2: 60052
LNER V2 2-6-2: 60831/5/65/919/57
LNER B1 4-6-0: 61029/76/99/244/78/344/50/
      61354/96
North British Rly J36 0-6-0: 65236
LNER J38 0-6-0: 65929
BR Class 4 2-6-0: 76105/9
BR Class 4 2-6-4T: 80003/55/122

Diesel
English Electric Type 4: D248/389
Brush Type 4: D1580
North British 200hp 0-4-0 shunter: D2705
North British 225hp 0-4-0 shunter: D2715/23/47
BR 350hp 0-6-0 shunter: D3736/40/1/880
Birmingham RC&W Type 2: D5307
Clayton Type 1: D8554/8/61/5/7/73
English Electric Type 5 Deltic: D9008

Total Steam: 26 Diesel: 19

failure in the Grantshouse area. There were two depots in this mining area, North Blyth which was a roundhouse situated on the north side of the River Blyth. The other was a six-road straight shed at South Blyth, on the south side of the river. To gain access to the North shed I used an old rope ferry service. I bunked both these sheds on Saturday 24th February, 1963. On both sheds I noted 29 steam locos and just three diesel shunters. I copped the lot. Sadly, the two sheds closed on 9th September, 1967 and 27th May, 1967 respectively. North Blyth was replaced by Cambois diesel depot but that too has now closed.

Today, in pouring rain and semi-darkness we were offered a lift to the area where the two sheds once stood. A young couple who had been travelling on the Edinburgh-Morpeth service drove us to where I hoped the Blyth coal shipping staithes would still be standing intact, but because of the rain-filled sky and the darkness of that night I really couldn't make out whether or not the staithes were there. The couple assured me they were.

We stayed in a very friendly b. & b. and all the people I spoke to concerning the staiths agreed that they were still there.

The next morning after we'd eaten a hearty breakfast, Ashleigh and I bade everyone at the b. & b. a fond farewell. On opening the front door I discovered that the rain was still teaming down. The 15-minute walk to Morpeth station was not the best way to start the day. However, we arrived at the station and soon found shelter in a warm waiting room.

I glanced out of the waiting room window and my eyes followed the raindrops as they trickled down the glass in the windows. Suddenly, a van arrived and parked in the station car park. I noticed a chap sitting inside reading a newspaper. The van had a name on it - Jarvis. I'd seen these vans on a number of occasions and I knew they were something to do with railway maintenance.

I wondered whether the van driver might have some information on the staithes. I advised Ashleigh that I was just nipping out to talk to him. I tapped gently on his widow and on observing me, he rolled the window open.

"Good morning," I said.

"Morning," he answered pleasantly.

"My name's Alex," I advised him. "I'm from Birmingham and I've been making enquiries about the Blyth staithes and if they're still standing," I concluded.

He shook my hand and then introduced himself. "My name's Keith and I live in Blyth and, yes, the staithes are still there." I must admit on hearing this news I was close to tears. I had only seen them on one occasion and that was on a very cold winter afternoon on Sunday 24th February, 1963. The whole country had entered a new year into one of the worst winters in our history.

My sombre thoughts on the staithes and my thoughts on my one and only visit to this area all those years ago were interrupted by Ashleigh calling me and advising that our train was approaching. "Dad, our train's approaching and there's a stack of people waiting for it," she called. I shook Keith's hand again then, turning, I headed towards my daughter who was standing close to the station entrance.

For the first time since we had left Birmingham in the early hours of Monday morning I felt an inner warmth. The thoughts that kept me warm as we journeyed southwards were the fact that the staithes were still there. I wanted to see the old steam sheds of yesteryear. I wanted to see the steam engines that gave me so much pleasure. I wanted to be with Melvin and David, scurrying around sheds, sidings and workshops. To see a Streak, Semi, Merchant Navy, Scot, Battle of Britain, Patriot, B1, Jubilee, A1, Clan, Schools, A2, Princess, A3 or a Britannia would have made my day.

I brushed away a tear as I turned and peered out of the window of the unit that was taking Ashleigh and me onwards to Newcastle. Suddenly, I felt Ashleigh's head touch my shoulder, she'd fallen off to sleep. The train glided past the modern depot at Heaton, the old shed was coded 52B. There were several sheds in this fantastic area - Blaydon, Tweedmouth, Percy Main, Consett, Tyne Dock, Gateshead. We were about to visit the latter two.

On arrival at Newcastle station, it was very evident that the past was firmly present. Some of the old platforms had disappeared, along with some of the old timers that probably spent their entire lives working on the railway. I'd have given anything for the sound of a steam locomotive's

Locomotives on Gateshead shed, 52A, 24th February, 1963

Steam

A4 4-6-2: 60002/5/16/20
A1 4-6-2: 60126/54
B1 4-6-0: 61019
K1 2-6-0: 62010/29
J39 0-6-0: 64701
J27 0-6-0: 65791/853/4
V3 2-6-2T: 67628/45/53/4/62/73/8
J94 0-6-0ST: 68053/9
J72 0-6-0T: 68736/69001/4/5/23/5

Total Steam: 28 Diesel: 48

Diesel

Sulzer Type 4 'Peak': D88/130/66/9/79/81/8/91
English Electric Type 4:
D240/1/5/7/51/6/70/4/5/346/63/92/3
Brush Type 4: D1502
BR 204hp 0-6-0 shunter: D2056/7/8/61/147
Drewry 204hp 0-6-0 shunter: D2311/2/3
Hunslet 204hp 0-6-0 shunter: D2594
BR 350hp 0-6-0 shunter: D3078/455
Sulzer Type 2: D5098/100/1/10/1/47/8/9/50/7/79
Birmingham RC&W Type 2: D5375
English Electric Type 3: D6785/6
English Electric Type 5 Deltic: D9019

whistle prior to departing this very famous station. I thought of an A4 pulling out on a crack express heading north or south. "What a mouthwatering idea," I thought as I stood there looking back in time.

The rain kept us company as we made our way over to Gateshead., and it followed us as we strolled around the old area where Tyne Dock once stood.

The shed at 52A Gateshead was derelict and it was a sad sight to see. I first bunked this depot on Sunday morning 24th February, 1963. The bad winter of that year had the whole country in its grip. It lasted until early April, 1963. I noted 28 steam locos on, including A4s Nos. 60002/5, 16 and

How sad Gateshead shed looked in April, 2000 compared with our January, 1963 visit when it was bustling with engines, steam and diesel. The shed is now closed completely and just two BR 350hp(Class 08) diesel shunters lay there derelict.
(Alex Scott)

20, and 48 diesels. I copped 59.

The shed closed to steam in October, 1965 but in its heyday it was truly massive and prior to 1956 consisted of four roundhouses and a specially built three-road straight shed to house the A4s. After '56 it was reduced to two roundhouses and a nine-road straight shed.

The walk over the River Tyne via the road bridge had my young daughter gasping as I pointed out to her all the bridges that were in the vicinity, including the famous King Edward bridge.

Tyne Dock, 52H, which had three enclosed roundhouses and a five-road straight shed closed on 9th September, 1967. Out of 54 engines seen I copped - 54. It's a housing estate now.

It was still raining when we left Newcastle for our journey back to Birmingham via York, Leeds, Bradford, Wakefield and Doncaster, visiting ex-depots along the way. I was rather saddened by the sights that greeted me. The depots that I and my school chums had bunked many many years ago had nearly all gone.

A little further down the line I bunked 52G Sunderland - the time was about 5am on that 1963 Sunday morning. The depot consisted of a straight shed and a small roundhouse. I noted 41 on and copped 41. Today. there's a couple of Jarvis Portakabins on site, plus some sidings.

The next depot was at 51A Darlington. All that was visible of this one-time vast area was a wasteland on the morning of Tuesday 17th April, 2000. But in the very early hours of Saturday morning 20th February, 1965 I was escorted part way from Yarm Road to the depot foreman's office by a young police constable. On our arrival, the gaffer made me smile after he sat in his chair listening to the officer's explanation of my presence. He said seriously: "You brought him, you take him round." In actual fact, that's exactly what he did do.

At approximately 2.35am the young constable and I bunked the shed. It

Locomotives on Darlington shed, 51A, 19th February, 1965

Steam

Fairburn Class 4 2-6-4T: 42085/194
Class 4 2-6-0: 43050/6/7/99/129
8F 2-8-0: 48283/344/92
V2 2-6-2: 60806/24/85
B1 4-6-0: 61216
K1 2-6-0: 62001/8/41/4/5/7/8/59
J27 0-6-0: 65842/57
J94 0-6-0ST: 68010/1/23/37/43/7/53/60
BR Class 4 4-6-0: 75021
WD 2-8-0: 90011/4/309/593/458

Diesel

English Electric Type 4: D328
BR 204hp 0-6-0 shunter: D2080
Drewry 204hp 0-6-0 shunter: D2206/31/308
Hunslet 204hp 0-6-0 shunter: D2607
BR 350hp 0-6-0 shunter: D3228/677

Total Steam: 38 Diesel: 8

was a very cold morning as we clambered around the seven-road straight shed and then into the old NER roundhouse. The depot had a good mixture on and I noted 48, of which I copped 27. The officer and I walked and talked all the time we were ambling around the two sheds. I think he really enjoyed himself.

We arrived back at Darlington Bank Top station just after 3am, I noted two old locomotives in the station, *Locomotion* and *Derwent*, The officer and I chatted for a while, then he left me to have a couple of hours kip in the warm waiting room. I remember a large coal fire glowing in the hearth as my eyes slowly closed and I fell asleep. A porter woke me up with a cuppa at 5.45am.

I'd already bunked 50A York en-route to Darlington. I'd also been apprehended by an engine driver on the authority of the depot foreman. Luckily I'd noted all the engines on shed and out in the yard before I was collared. I was taken to the forman's office and after giving me a barrage of abuse, he very kindly handed me a cup of tea, a sandwich and a couple of fairy cakes. To my utter surprise, he turned to me and after noticing I'd eaten my snap he told me to leave. Actually, he didn't say "leave," it was more

Locomotives on York shed, 50A, 10th February, 1963

Steam

Class 5 2-6-0: 42900
Ivatt Class 4 2-6-0: 43014/71/97/126
Class 5 4-6-0: 44728
A4 4-6-2: 60016
A3 4-6-2: 60039/54/91
A1 4-6-2: 60121/4/38/46/50/3/5
A2 4-6-2: 60518
V2 2-6-2: 60810/31/3/7/55/6/64/76/7/8/86/7/95/924/5/9/39/67/8/74/5/81/2
B1 4-6-0: 61002/12/31/53/198/229/73/6/365/78
B16 4-6-0: 61434/55/7
K1 2-6-0: 62005/9/38/46/9/54/6/7/61
O4 2-8-0: 63576
J27 0-6-0: 65844/9/94
BR Class 3 2-6-0: 77012
WD 2-8-0: 90030/424/67/97/571/623/54/63
9F 2-10-0: 92137/200

Diesel

English Electric Type 4: D258/9/76/8/82/3/346/7/8/9/50/5/85/90
BR 204hp 0-6-0 shunter: D2062/5/6/75/161
Drewery 204hp 0-6-0 shunter: D2245/68/9/70
BR 350hp 0-6-0 shunter: D3071/239/40/314/5/9/20/874
English Electric Type 1: D8011

Total

Steam: 78
Diesel: 32

like "f*** off." So I did, the driver laughing at me as I slid past him.

I noted 26 on, copped 26 plus I'd had some tea, a sandwich and two small but very tasty fairy cakes.

Today, it is totally different. There are no locomotives to see, nor any foreman hurling abuse and then offering me some of his lunch. The National Railway Museum now occupies the former twin roundhouse and straight shed. Two of the four roundhouses were replaced by the straight shed in the 1950s. The shed closed to steam in June, 1967 and the remaining roundhouse became the museum in the 1970s. The straight shed closed altogether in the 1980s and is now part of the museum. Oh, how I wish I was sitting in the foreman's office just for old time's sake.

We were now heading off on a local service to another area of interest, Bradford. On Saturday 20th February, 1965 I bunked three depots in this area. The first was out at 56G Hammerton Street. The depot was situated a good three quarters of a mile from Bradford Exchange station and a brisk 15-minute walk found me strolling around the diesel depot. I noted eight shunters on and copped five. The depot closed in 1984 and today a bus garage stands on the site.

Ashleigh and I hurried over to Bradford Forster Square station and were looking for a Halifax service when we were approached by a railwayman. He asked us which train we were about to board. I had my shed directory in my hand and he may have noticed me reading it prior to boarding.

"We're off to Halifax in the hope of seeing the old steam shed at 56F Low Moor," I advised him.

"I can help you there," he stated. "It closed in 1967. A tram museum was housed in the former six-road steam shed but it proved totally unsuccessful. They stable buses in there now and it's protected by security guards."

"No point going then," I said.

"No, not really," he agreed.

I later discovered that the information he gave me was not entirely correct. Nothing remains of the shed which closed in October, 1967 and the site is waste ground which has recently been landscaped. The tram museum was built on the opposite side of the Bradford-Halifax line, on the site of the goods yard and carriage sidings. The rest, about the museum being unsuccessful, the buses and security guards was true. We were at the wrong station for Halifax, anyway.

"There used to be another shed in this area," I added.

"Yes, it was at Manningham," said the railwayman. "It's a large industrial estate now." A short pause as he thought about telling me where it was situated. "Yes, it's on the right hand side just after the small road bridge, and on the opposite side is a large waste disposal area. I'm working the Leeds service via Shipley and I'll blow the horn on the unit when we pass

Locomotives on Bradford Manningham shed, 55F, 19th February, 1965

Steam

Fairburn Class 4 2-6-4T: 42072/189
Ivatt Class 4 2-6-0: 43016/30/51/74
BR Clan 4-6-2: 72009
BR Class 3 2-6-0: 77001

Diesel

BR 204hp 0-6-0 shunter: D2044/61/5/71

Total   Steam: 8   Diesel: 4

it," he finally concluded. I peered out of the window in anticipation and when I heard the horn sound, into view came a large industrial estate and, on the opposite side, a waste disposal area.

On arrival in Leeds we set about finding our way over to 55H Neville Hill. We weren't allowed access to the depot but were informed that it worked around the clock servicing and fuelling 125s and Northern Spirit units. We were also advised that there were three class 08 shunters in the depot area, 08950, 08588 and what looked like 08567. The last time I visited this depot there were 21 locos on and I copped two. In the early years, the shed had four roundhouses and it closed to steam on 12th June, 1967.

The next depot I visited on Saturday 20th February, 1965 was out at 56A, Wakefield. The L&YR depot was a 10-road straight shed and on that particular day I noted 83 on plus some locos I can't really recall, but I did note them. They included London Tilbury & Southend 4-4-2T *Thundersley,* an engine named *Seagull,* Midland 4-2-2 No. 118 and Midland 2-4-0 No. 145A. The depot closed on 3rd January, 1967, becoming wagon repair shops until final closure in 1988. I was advised that the shed was demolished a few years ago leaving an open space.

I bunked several depots around Leeds and the North East but I lost a very valuable note pad in 1966 so I have no proof that I visited the following, though I know I did: 51J Northallerton, 55A Leeds Holbeck, 55B Stourton, 55C Farnley Junction, 55D Royston, 55E Normanton, 56B Ardsley and 56C Copley Hill.

On passing Northallerton there was nothing visible. At Holbeck, a firm of private railway maintenance contractors, Jarvis, use the site as a depot for track maintenance machines. There is a Freightliner terminal at Stourton, wasteland at Farnley Junction, Normanton, Royston and Ardsley where the M1 passes over the site on a bridge. At Copley Hill, Lye Spencer have a steel warehouse on the steam shed site.

We boarded the King's Cross service at Wakefield Westgate. Our next depot was at Retford, 36E. The only time I ever bunked this depot was on a Sunday afternoon, 17th February, 1963. There were 15 steam locos on and one 0-6-0 diesel shunter, No. D3443. I took several photos and they all turned out. I copped eleven. Today, Simon Reeve Rental occupy the shed

Locomotives noted on Retford shed, 36E, 17th February, 1963

Steam

Ivatt Class 4 2-6-0: 43127
B1 4-6-0: 61055/127/1208/12/13/25
K1 2-6-0: 62019
O4 2-8-0: 63718/30/71/914
O2 2-8-0: 63934/9/66

Diesel

BR 350hp 0-6-0 shunter: D3443

Total Steam: 15 Diesel: 1

Class B1 4-6-0 No. 61208 was one of 15 steam locos on Retford shed when we bunked it on 17th February, 1963. *(Alex Scott)*

and they deal in mobile trolleys. Also in the vicinity are three old brick buildings that were obviously part of the steam depot's amenity blocks.

We returned to Doncaster on the first available service and on arrival we soon found the MacDonalds so I treated Ashleigh to a burger, chips and sparkling Coke. The train to Sheffield took us via Mexborough. I never bunked this massive 15-road straight shed but I, along with Melvin and David, passed it en-route to Donny on a couple of occasions.

Today there's nothing to see. The metal overbridge still stands the test of time but the guard advised me that work was in progress to build an underpass and the bridge will soon be taken out and cut up at C. F. Booth's scrap metal company just outside Rotherham Central station.

The next depot we passed en-route to Sheffield was Grimesthorpe. I only visited this roundhouse once and that was on Sunday 3rd March, 1963. It closed to steam on 11th September, 1961 but there were 31 diesels stabled

Above: Also on Retford shed on 17th February, 1963 was Class O4/8 2-8-0 No. 63718. The O4s were introduced by the Great Central Railway in 1911 but quite a few were later rebuilt in various forms. Rebuilding into Class O4/8 with the then standard B1 boiler commenced in 1944. *(Alex Scott)*

Below: Retford shed on 18th April, 2000. Closed on 14th June, 1965 the building and yard are now used by Simon Reeve, container rental. *(Alex Scott)*

there. I copped 14. Today, a shopping precinct covers part of the area.

The shed out at Millhouse was never bunked by me although we passed it several times en-route to Sheffield and Doncaster. It was an eight-road straight shed of Midland origin and closed on 1st January, 1962. It is used for industrial and retail purposes today.

The shed at Hasland 18C was situated a few miles south of Chesterfield station. I only bunked this old Midland roundhouse once but again I have no proof. Today, as we passed the site heading towards Birmingham, I noticed that the entire area was an overgrown wasteland. The depot was closed on 7th September, 1964.

The next depot was 17A Derby. This shed was always bunked by the lads and me. The works lay next-door to the old Midland roundhouse and we always bunked that as well.

The shed area was very vast and every time we passed it en-route to Nottingham it stretched for miles and miles. A small diesel loco servicing shed remains, otherwise a handful of coaches rest on the site while what's left of the once huge loco works is now owned by ADtranz.

The 125 crept out of Derby station with Ashleigh and me on board. The rain outside was still falling and gently trickling down the windows. The darkness of another day slowly moved overhead as our train headed towards Burton. The day was gradually coming to an end. I honestly can't visualise me ever again visiting the areas I've just been to.

As the train rolled into a rain-soaked New Street station, my thoughts were on the trips that I and my two school chums made over 36 years ago. Funny really, they all seem like yesterday. The trips were fantastic and the depot foremen that we accidentally bumped into while trying to bunk in, bunk round and eventually slip out in ghostly fashion had me smiling to myself as passengers clambered on and off the 125 to Plymouth.

The last train ride on that wet evening found us at Duddeston. My wife Carol met us and we called into the fish and chip shop before arriving home from our trip back in time. I must say that I did enjoy it, although there wasn't much to see at times. It's the adventure and not knowing what's there, just like all those years ago in those great days of steam.

There are three key areas I've still to visit before I finally conclude revisiting those great depots that once upon a time held us spell-bound with mysterious, marvellous, magnificent moments in time. I'll be covering the North West, plus three sheds in Liverpool, the depots in and around Manchester, the various sheds in London and, finally, the last outpost, Weymouth. I'll be revisiting the depots en-route to Weymouth within the coming weeks but for now it's time to say goodnight.

THE WARMTH OF AN APRIL MORNING

The sun shone down on us as we headed off to visit my parents' grave in the quaint old holiday resort of Bognor Regis. My mother died first, on 25th June, 1987; she was buried on 1st July. My father died on 29th February, 1988 and he was buried on 8th March. They're buried together and rest peacefully in another world where the sun shines down on them and the worries of this world are non-existent.

We called in at Eastleigh depot en-route. I felt it was going to be a day of remembering family, friends and history. My family consisted of my mom - Joan - my dad - Billy - and my sister - Sheila. The two friends were, of course, Melvin and David. The history of times past and friends remembered seemed to go hand-in-hand at this moment.

The smell of simmering smoke rising skywards, coal tenders full to capacity and water dripping gently out of a Merchant Navy, a Schools or a small 0-6-0 tank had me crying and wanting to touch the past with a heavy heart. I could hear Melvin's voice echoing around the yard as he advised me where to go and where to meet up after I'd collected all the loco numbers.

My wife and Ashleigh sat in the car enjoying a short break while I walked around in the shadows of yesterday. The steam engines that were once in abundance at this great Southern stronghold are only pleasant memories to me, but I did manage to bunk the shed for old time sake and I took a few photos, just as I did on that wintry day of Sunday 30th January, 1965.

Merchant Navy class Pacific No. 35020 *Bibby Line* at Eastleigh shed on 30th January, 1965. *(Alex Scott)*

USA class 0-6-0T No. 30073 on shunting duty at Eastleigh shed, 30th January, 1965. These engines were classed USA because they were brought over from America during the second world war. After the war, they passed to the Southern Railway which used them for shunting at Southampton Docks, among other things. *(Alex Scott)*

Merchant Navy 4-6-2 No. 35002 *Union Castle* at Eastleigh shed on 30th January, 1965. *(Alex Scott)*

Locomotives on Eastleigh shed, 71A, 9th December, 1962

Steam

28xx 2-8-0: 2890
57xx 0-6-0PT: 4616/56/8799
43xx 2-6-0: 7327
Manor 4-6-0: 7823
T9 4-4-0: 120
M7 0-4-4T: 30032/36/45/131/3/480
USA 0-6-0T: 30064/5
B4 0-4-0T: 30101
O2 0-4-4T: 30199/225
G16 4-8-0T: 30494/5
S15 4-6-0: 30497/502/12/5/840
H15 4-6-0: 30522
Q class 0-6-0: 30530/2/3/42/3
700 class 0-6-0: 30695
King Arthur 4-6-0: 30770
Schools 4-4-0: 30903/12/29/37
Z class 0-8-0T: 30953/4
N class 2-6-0: 31404/14/816
U class 2-6-0: 31613/9/21/5/39/791/3/804/9
U1 class 2-6-0: 31892
W class 2-6-4T: 31913
K class 2-6-0: 32344/6/9/50/1/2
E6 0-6-2T: 32408
Q1 0-6-0: 33001/2/7/39
West Country 4-6-2: 34016/21/2/31/4/8/98

Battle of Britain 4-6-2: 34073
Merchant Navy 4-6-2: 35011
Ivatt Class 2 2-6-2T: 41293/305/11/9/25/8/9
Fairburn 2-6-4T: 42112
BR Class 5 4-6-0: 73002/16/7/20/41/65/86/9/110/2/4/9
BR Class 4 4-6-0: 75065
BR Class 4 2-6-0: 76010/1/6/29/57/8/60/1/2/3/4/8/9/89
BR Class 4 2-6-4T: 80043/65/6/82/3
BR Class 2 2-6-2T: 82012/4/5/6
9F 2-10-0: 92205/6/31/9
Crosti 9F 2-10-0: 92029

Diesel

Drewry 204hp 0-6-0 shunter: D2254/89
Birmingham RC&W Type 3: D6504/6/8/20/30/2/3/46/56/83
BR 350hp 0-6-0 shunter: D3012/4/15230/2/3/4/5/6

Total Steam: 121 Diesel: 20

A refreshing cup of coffee before we departed and stopped just a few yards up the road opposite the main entrance to the works. The old BR entrance is still there but it's closed and visitors have to use gate number two. The area is still massive and when we bunked it we were certainly lucky that day. I could only see a couple of railway employees working in the yard. Sadly, there was no beautiful Merchant Navy class loco glistening in the sunshine, no Battle of Britains quietly boasting their new paintwork.

Oh for the sight of a named Standard class 5 basking in its glorious emerald green. The thought of a party awaiting entry to the works had me smiling to myself. I wanted someone just to turn up with pad and pen if only to complete the picture, but sadly not an engine spotter in sight.

On passing the station on my right, I recall a softly-spoken lady announcing the imminent passage of the through boat train from Southampton Terminus to Waterloo. She advised passengers to "stand clear on platform 3, the approaching service is non-stop to London Waterloo."

Melvin, David and myself had our backs against the brick waiting room wall as the train flashed through the station. I remember how the whole station shuddered. We did manage to get the number of the B-o-B as she hauled the immaculate rake of clean, green coaches through the station. Today, the only trains that scurry through are freight trains hauled by class 37s, 47s and 66s.

On arrival at the graveside, I knelt close to the heads of my parents' gravestone. I talked about my children and what they had accomplished since our last visit. Within seconds of my arrival I felt tears of sadness gently rolling down my face. After a while it was time to turn for home. I kissed the stone of history and with a very heavy heart bade them farewell, saying: "I love and miss you both very much. Oh, and thankyou for lighting the fire of my life, see ya one day."

Locomotives in Eastleigh Works 9th December, 1962

Steam

57xx 0-6-0PT: 4634/9756
B4 0-4-0T: 30102
S15 4-6-0: 30499/500/837/42
Z class 0-8-0T: 30957
U class 2-6-0: 31636/800
N class 2-6-0: 31843/73
U1 class 2-6-0: 31897
A1x 0-6-0T: 32661
Q1 0-6-0: 33010/2/25/38
West Country 4-6-2: 34007/39/46/70/93
Battle of Britain 4-6-2: 34052/72/80/1/8
Merchant Navy 4-6-2: 35009/21
Ivatt Class 2 2-6-2T: 41296
BR Class 5 4-6-0: 73018/81/115/8
BR Class 4 4-6-0: 75029
BR Class 4 2-6-0: 76006/55
BR Class 4 2-6-4T: 80037/94
BR Class 3 2-6-2T: 82019/24

Diesel

BR 350hp 0-6-0 shunter: D3097/221/6/15215
Birmingham RC&W Type 3: D6515/8/9/25

Electric

BR 2,552hp Bo-Bo: E5024

Total Steam: 42   Diesel: 9 Electric: 1

WE WEREN'T EXACTLY SINGING IN THE RAIN

I'd set the alarm for 4.30am but I hardly slept through that particular night of Monday 24th April, 2000. Ashleigh and I were due to be out of the house at 5.15 for the bus to town at 5.25. The train to Liverpool left New Street at 06.20.

I was wide awake when the alarm went off dead on time. The excitement of another trip had kept me awake nearly all night. However, I was awake and up just like I was in the days when the lads and I travelled mile after mile collecting steam engines and diesels.

I had prepared everything for our trip the night before. It was just a case of making up some tasty sandwiches and a flask of coffee, plus a packet of Jammie Dodgers. Ashleigh sat at the breakfast table crunching on her cornflakes while I tucked into beans on double toast. This was washed down with a mug of coffee.

The clock displayed 5.15am and it was time to leave but the most important thing I'd forgotten to do before leaving was to check the weather. I peeped through the curtain and mumbled: "Sod it, it's pouring down."

We only waited a few seconds at the bus stop before the bus duly arrived. We boarded, paid our fares then sat down and gazed out of the window. The early morning monsoon raged fiercely outside. At approximately 5.47 we arrived in town. Then we hurried over to New Street to check the departure board.

The train was on platform 5b. We boarded and awaited departure. I had a word with the guard and explained what we were about to do travel-wise. He was great and said: "I can't see any restrictions for you to travel to Carnforth via Liverpool." I was really relieved that we could go that way because I wanted to revisit Bank Hall, Walton-on-the-Hill and Edge Hill.

I returned to my seat and found Ashleigh fast asleep. The rain continued all the way to Lime Street. On arrival, we made our way down to the underground and alighted at the Central station where we joined another service to 27A Bank Hall. I bunked this shed with Melvin during the summer hols of '62 but I have no proof because I lost my pad in '66.

On arrival at Bank Hall I noticed several small swimming pools had formed in several key areas on the uneven platform. Ashleigh and I scampered up the rain-soaked stairs which led us out of the station. We were just about to follow the route to the shed according to my shed directory when I heard someone call out: "Tickets." I spun round and noticed a chap inside the ticket office.

I opened my glasses case and was just about to show him our tickets when he smiled and said: "Sorry, I wasn't talking to you. I was talking to the chap who had purchased his tickets and walked off without picking them up."

I put the tickets back in my glasses case, then put my case back in my inside coat pocket. Once again, I was studying the route to 27A. I felt that the chap in the ticket office was watching me. I could see him out of the corner of my eye.

"I haven't seen one of those books in donkey's years," he stated. The office door opened and he came out and looked at the book.

"I used to be a driver at Bank Hall shed," he informed us. "There's nothing there, only grass. The old steam shed used to be just over that wall." I peered over the wall and all that was visible was grass, a rather lush looking piece, I might add.

"Walton-on-the Hill," he said. "That depot closed, ermm, now what year was it?" He paused and thought for a while, then added: "Yes, it was a six-road straight shed. It closed in 1963. There's some houses there now, and I believe the line from the junction has long gone."

I listened to his every word then I thought it a waste of time going back to Sandhills station, changing trains and heading off to Walton.

"The other shed was over at Edge Hill. Now that one was massive. There must have been at least 19 roads at the straight shed. Unfortunately, it closed some time in May, 1968," he finally concluded. At that point he handed me my directory and returned to the office.

The rain continued as we headed back to Liverpool Lime Street. On arrival, we boarded a local service to Wigan. On passing the site of the former steam depot at Edge Hill, we could clearly see the land had been unused since the days of steam. On passing Wigan loco, I noted the same locomotives in and around the shed area that were there on our last visit. Strange really, it was as if time had stood still.

The platform at Wigan was littered with youngsters all heading off to Blackpool for the day. I heard some of them chatting about certain rides they were going to go on. The Liverpool-Blackpool service was announced as a class 66 hurried through heading north. The Blackpool train arrived and we were lucky to get seats as it was packed.

On arrival at Preston station, we soon found the all-stations service to Colne, stopping at Lostock Hall. We departed at 10.50 and arrived at 10.56. Ashleigh was quick to point at 66137, running light. Once outside the station we soon found derelict land. The one-time eight-road straight shed had long gone. It closed its doors to steam on 5th August, 1968, one of the last steam depots on BR.

The last time I visited Lostock Hall was on a spring Sunday morning, 28th March, 1965. I noted 40 mixed locos on including two Brits., 70024 and 70049. I copped 10.

Locomotives on Lostock Hall shed, 10D, 28th March, 1965

Steam

Fairburn Class 4 2-6-4T: 42158/87/286
Stanier Class 4 2-6-4T: 42436/625
Class 5 4-6-0: 44678/816/902/4/5045/129/226/425
LMS 3F 0-6-0T: 47293/317/36/62/454/584
8F 2-8-0: 48039/307/400/18/34/8/707/30
Britannia 4-6-2: 70024/49
BR Class 2 2-6-0: 78002/22/37/41/57
WD 2-8-0: 90354/60/720

Diesel

Yorkshire Engine Co. 179hp 0-4-0 shunter: D2862
BR 350hp 0-6-0 shunter: D3581

Total

Steam: 37
Diesel: 2

What remained of Lostock Hall shed in the year 2000. The shed roads can still be clearly seen. *(Alex Scott)*

The train back to Preston was running very late. When it arrived I noticed the guard helping a chap who was disabled. I have every sympathy for these people and I've always assisted them if I felt they needed it, but this chap delayed the train for six minutes. He was asking the guard all manner of questions about the station: "Is there a lift? Can someone assist me to a telephone? Anyone got change for a five pound note?" I was becoming a little annoyed at this situation that I felt should have been dealt with prior to his journey.

Our next port of call was Lancaster and the timing of that service worried me because we only had a few minutes to get our connection from Preston. It was in and awaiting departure as our train finally came to rest in Preston. Within seconds we were running hell-for-leather over the bridge and only made it with seconds to spare, in fact the guard was just disappearing into the back cab of the unit.

We slumped into the first available seats. My heart was beating ten to the dozen. The guard smiled at us as he came round clipping the tickets and he only said one word to us: "Lucky." I handed him our tickets which he duly clipped after inspection. We had a quick bite to eat and a sip of pop before we arrived at another rain-soaked station, Lancaster.

I only visited this oddly designed depot on one occasion and that was on Sunday 27th February, 1966. I have no record of what was on but today we followed the shed directory and we found a Sainsburys store on the site of the former locomotive depot. The shed was a four-road straight shed with all the roads leading from a turntable. It closed on 18th April, 1966, just two months after my visit. The only reason I can come up with about not noting any locomotives on this shed is that there may not have been any!

The rain continued all the way to our next place of interest, Carnforth. I bunked this six-road straight shed on 29th February, 1966. I noted 28 on. These included some Ivatt 2-6-0s, Stanier Black Five 4-6-0s and 8F 2-8-0s, Standard 4-6-0s and a couple of diesels including loco No. D5700. I copped this loco which was built by Metropolitan Vickers and introduced in 1958.

Ashleigh and I strolled around the old steam shed. I observed a variety of

Carnforth shed on 25th April, 2000. Still intact at the time of writing and used by the West Coast Railway Company for locomotives, steam and diesel, and coaches. *(Alex Scott)*

132

coaches that had been strategically arranged for the benefit of whom? The coal and ash plants towered over us like gods. There was a handful of diesel locomotives spread around the shed area which included 03196, 08220, 37248 in need of urgent repair, and I noted two class 08s in the yard close to the signal box. Loco number 66016 hurried through heading north.

We awaited the local service back to Lancaster, then another local to another shed. The next two depots were bunked on Sunday 28th March, 1965. Lower Darwen 10H and Rose Grove 10F. On Lower Darwen I noted 24 mixed locos and copped seven on the old L&YR eight-road straight shed that closed on 14th February, 1966 to become just wasteland.

Over at Rose Grove I noted 25 including several 2-8-0s. I copped eight on this six-road straight shed that was one of the last working steam depots in the country, the others being Carnforth and Lostock Hall. Today it's underneath the M56.

I visited a number of depots in this area on that particular Sunday, including Warrington, Wigan and Fleetwood which I have already written about. The other depots visited were Bury, Bolton, Agecroft, Patrifcroft, Newton Heath and Trafford Park. The only place with any railway interest in modern times was Bury, 9M. The eight-road straight shed was closed on 12th April, 1965 and was pulled down some years later. Today, the electric car shops remain and they are used by the East Lancashire Railway.

A housing estate now stands on the site of the former 12-road straight shed at Bolton. Agecroft is being redeveloped soon. Patricroft is an industrial estate but it housed 45 locomotives in and around the L-shaped area which comprised an eight-road straight shed and a smaller building.

Trafford Park is now a Freightliner terminal and on my final visit to this massive 20-road straight shed before its closure on 4th March, 1968 it had 36 on. I managed to cop eight.

Another massive Manchester shed was over at Newton Heath. I noted 72 mixed locomotives on this sprawling 23-road straight shed which was the largest depot on the L&Y Railway. I copped 13. Today, it's used by First North Western and maintains nearly all its rolling stock.

A very tricky shed was Gorton. I only bunked it on one occasion but once again I have no proof. The shed foreman was really great to Melvin, David and me on that Sunday many years ago. I remember it as if it was yester-

Locomotives on Bury shed, 9M, 28th March, 1965

Class 5 2-6-0: 42855
4F 0-6-0: 44311
Ivatt Class 2 2-6-0: 46405/6/12/4/6/7/36/9/501/4/6
Class 5 4-6-0: 45104/252/318/77/81/415
8F 2-8-0: 48100/373/469   ***Total*** Steam: 22   No diesels

Closed in 1965, Bury steam shed is long gone but the old workshops once used to maintain the electric trains that ran betwen Bury and Manchester now form a steam shed and workshop for the East Lancashire Railway. (Alex Scott)

day because some lads from down south were really being abusive to him because he refused them entry into his shed.

As we approached this small gathering of abusive spotters, we heard them calling the foreman everything under the sun. I thought at the time that we had no chance of getting in because of this unfortunate situation we had stumbled into. However, we bided our time and once these lads had cleared off Melvin spoke to the foreman, no doubt playing his sympathy classic. It worked every time. A young fireman took us round. A market now occupies the area.

The rain continued as we headed back to Manchester Piccadilly. On arrival we boarded the train to Birmingham via Stoke. En-route I noticed 66022, 66035 and 66092. We were rerouted via Bescot and there I noted 66176, 66215, 67017 and 87007 in the shed area. Odd really that the last engine we would see as the curtain came down on another trip down Memory Lane was 87007 *City of Manchester*.

I've counted all the locos that Ashleigh and I have seen today, Tuesday 25th April, 2000. It comes to a very poor 32. On that fantastic North West tour on Sunday 28th March, 1965 I noted 468 on the 12 sheds I visited. Unbelievable. I copped a grand total of 111.

THE END OF THE LINE

It seems like only yesterday when I first set out to write about what replaced, if anything, those former steam sheds that I along with Melvin, David, Spinner, Eamon, Gerry, Nicky, John, Martin and the unforgettable little Kevin bunked all those years ago. I've seen Spinner on the odd occasion but I've never seen any of the other lads since those carefree days way back in the Swinging Sixties. I often wonder where they are today and, on reflection, whether I should have kept in touch.

Ashleigh and I are about to set off on the final trip but one down Memory Lane. I know we'll witness some special sights and no doubt I'll feel a tugging on my heart strings as I venture around those depots. The sights and sounds of the past will keep me company in the same way that all the lads did as we ventured nationwide in a bid to note as many steam locos as possible.

The first shed en-route to Weymouth will be Leamington Spa 84D. Ashleigh and I have arrived very early on Monday 31st July, 2000. With my trusty directory in hand we made our way to the four-road straight shed that Spinner and I bunked on a wintry Saturday afternoon, 9th February, 1963. We were pleased then to see a handful on, including 6016 *King Edward V*. Sadly, the brick-built depot closed on 14th June, 1965. Today, we are greeted by a familiar sight, an industrial estate.

Locomotives on Leamington Spa shed, 84D, Sat. 9th February, 1963

2251 0-6-0: 3217
5101 2-6-2T: 4118/25/33/71/5101
Castle 4-6-0: 5063
King 4-6-0: 6016
57xx 0-6-0PT: 7734
56xx 0-6-2T: 6671
Ivatt Class 2 2-6-2T: 41231
BR Class 4 4-6-0: 75000   ***Total*** Steam: 12   No diesels

We hurried back to Leamington Spa station and on arrival we quickly boarded the first service to Banbury 84C. This was another small four-road brick built straight shed. It closed on 3rd October, 1966. This is where Melvin, David and myself were caught by the shed foreman as we departed after successfully bunking his shed very late and under cover of darkness on a bitter cold night of Sunday 9th December, 1962. After a lengthy ticking-off he let us go, but only after he had dubbed us Fearless Ghosts. Today, only barren land greets our eyes as I stand looking at the past with fond memories of my good old school chums M. and D.

Locomotives on Banbury shed, 84C, 1st December, 1962

Steam
14xx 0-4-2T: 1440/55
2251 0-6-0: 2289
28xx 2-8-0: 2845/3806/9/15
5101 2-6-2T: 4105/12/54
61xx 2-6-2T: 6129
43xx 2-6-0: 6317/67
Castle 4-6-0: 5022/7033
King 4-6-0: 6027
Grange 4-6-0: 6812
Hall 4-6-0: 5912/26/6904/52/7912/5
72xx 2-8-2T: 7236
Class 5 4-6-0: 45222
8F 2-8-0: 48627
WD 2-8-0: 90065/483/5
9F 2-10-0: 92228

Diesel
BR 350hp 0-6-0 shunter: D3105/8

Total
Steam: 30
Diesel: 2

The local from Banbury took Ashleigh and me on to another small four-road straight shed that was actually a wooden structure, Oxford 81F. Sadly, the depot closed on 3rd January, 1966. Today, there's nothing visual but on the approach side of the station there's a small fuelling point and stabling sidings for Thames Trains sets. There were 50 locos on on that wintry Sunday night in '62.

At Oxford shed hosting Britannia 4-6-2 No. 70010 *Owen Glendower* **on 30th January, 1965.** (*Alex Scott*)

Engines and Eamon Crawley at Didcot shed, Sunday 25th October, 1964.
Above: BR Standard Class 5 4-6-0: 73024.*(Alex Scott)*
Below: Modified Hall 4-6-0 No. 6996 *Blackwell Hall* outside the shed.*(Alex scott)*

Another local to Didcot 81E. We were surprised to see a four-road straight shed with engines in and around the shed. In the yards I noted 09001, 58021, 60021, 60008 and 37375. What appeared to be a Swindon-built GWR railcar was at the old shed.

My thoughts turned to that unforgettable Sunday afternoon, 25th October, 1964, when I, along with Tony "Spinner" Jones, Eamon Crawley and Nicky "The Bounce" Hand bunked this depot. I took several photos of Eamon. Today, inside the shed I note with some sadness, several   locomotives that really and truly hurt my feelings. Notable among them is Castle class No. 5051 *Earl Bathurst*.

I have a photograph of David Burrows standing alongside this engine on Neath Court Sart depot. I also noted inside Didcot depot an 0-6-0ST, Cardiff Railway class engine No. 1338. I took a photo of this engine on the same day, at Swansea East Dock, oh so many years ago. The other locomotives in the shed are as follows: 3738, 4866, 6697, 60532, 5900, 7808, 6998, 6024, 5572, 1363, a diesel shunter named *Phantom*, No. 604 plus a works engine, No.11, a 75-ton crane and a wide variety of coaching stock.

We then headed for Swindon on board a late-running Paddington-Bristol service, en-route passing 66037 hauling an aggregates train. On arrival, we found 08856 on shunting duties and 66107 stood in the yard. The shed and works were gone. In their place now stands a museum, the Swindon Outlet Village, Arkells Brewery, the Turn Table pub and a multitude of shops, restaurants and stores.

Didcot shed, still full of steam locos on 31st July, 2000. Thanks to the Great Western Society I can relive my bunking days. The shed is much as it was then, only the locos are a hell of a lot cleaner! *(Alex Scott)*

The four of us bunked both Swindon shed and works on that memorable Sunday afternoon, 25th October, 1964. I recorded 48 on the shed and 96 on the works. The most notable locomotive in the cutting up area was none other than King class No. 6000 *King George V*. We were advised by an engine driver who just happened by that the engine was due to be cut up for scrap.

A Great Western 125 took Ashleigh and me on to Reading and on arrival we made our way to the old steam shed, coded 81D. It was a nine-road straight shed with four through roads. I only bunked this depot on one

`Locomotives on Reading South, 25th November, 1962

Steam

Schools 4-4-0: 30930
U class 2-6-0: 31617/797
N class 2-6-0: 31858/61/72
Q1 0-6-0: 33004

Diesel

Drewry 204hp 0-6-0 shunter: D2285
BR 350hp 0-6-0 shunter: D3048

BR Standard class 4 4-6-0 No. 75076 on Reading South - a sub-shed of 70C Guildford - 30th January, 1965. *(Alex Scott)*

occasion but I've no proof. The shed closed on 4th January, 1965. Today, several buildings occupy the former steam shed area along with a fuelling point and a service area for track machines.

On the eve of the bad winter 1962/63 Melvin, David and I got caught up in a severe snowstorm while en-route to Southall via Guildford and Feltham. We just had enough time to bunk Reading South. I photographed engine No. 31861, a class N. I recall bunking this depot on another occasion, Sunday 30th January, 1965. There were three steam and two diesel locos on the small three-road straight shed which closed some time that month. I took photos of loco 31809 and BR class 4 No. 75076.

Today, a rather large office block stands in the wake of the former sub-shed. It's called The Enegis Building. Close by are branches of Comet and Staples.

Ashleigh and I went on to Slough where a car park awaited our pleasure. I have no proof that I ever bunked this shed. However, I believe we would have bunked it at some time during our train spotting trips.

We returned to the station and boarded another local service to Southall. The shed here contained a variety of coaching stock, including some well-preserved Pullman stock. There were several old, rusting locomotive boilers awaiting attention outside in the yard. On Sunday afternoon, 25th November, 1962 the lads and I were pleased to observe an excellent mixture of both steam and diesel on shed. In fact, I noted 42 steam engines and 20 diesels.

Ashleigh and I boarded another local service into Paddington. Sadly, we weren't greeted by a Castle, Hall or a King awaiting departure to the West Country or Birkenhead via Snow Hill. Today, we observed so many individual trains that instead of taking notes we scurried towards the Underground and we were now heading off to our first Southern Region depot, 75D Stewarts Lane. I only ever bunked this shed on one occasion

Locomotives on Stewart's Lane shed, 75D, 24th March, 1963

Steam
Q class 0-6-0: 30534/7
Schools 4-4-0: 30928
H class 0-4-4T: 31305/542
N class 2-6-0: 31412/823/4/5/32/54/93
N1 class 2-6-0: 31822/77/8/9/80
U1 class 2-6-0: 31894/6
K class 2-6-0: 32337/40/3/7
Ivatt Class 4 2-6-0: 43121
BR class 4 4-6-0: 75069/70/4
BR Class 4 2-6-4T: 80012/34/68/81/5

Diesel
Drewry 204hp 0-6-0 shunter: D2277
BR 350hp 0-6-0 shunter: D3224
Birmingham RC&W Type 3: D6580
SR CC Type 4: 20001/2/3

Electric
BR 2,552hp Bo-Bo: E5003/6/15/21
Electro-Diesel Bo-Bo: E6001/5

Total   Steam: 32   Diesel: 6   Electric: 6

and that was after the steam shed closed some time in September, 1963. I noted nine diesels on.

Today, only a handful of diesels were visible plus some old coaching stock. The old entrance still remained, but any thoughts we had of bunking in were soon dispelled by a security guard who looked at us somewhat surprised. The depot had officially closed in October, 1997, so we were told. The one engine number I did manage to see was 73213. A private firm had taken over but the security guard wouldn't mention the firm's name.

The next depot we visited was over at 73C Hither Green'. On Sunday afternoon 16th August, 1964 I bunked this depot. A total of 24 mixed diesels were on. The shed closed its doors to steam long before I arrived, 39 years ago in October, 1961. Today, I noted several classes on the site of the old steam shed. They included class 08s, 09s, 59s, 60s, 66s and 73s.

We quickly ran back to the station where on arrival we headed off to Waterloo via London Bridge. The train rattled past Covent Garden, the home of another fantastic depot, Nine Elms, 70A. My two school chums and I bunked this depot on Sunday afternoon 1st July, 1962 and I noted 80 steam locos on and just six diesels. I copped 51.

The depot consisted of two adjoining buildings. The old shed was a 15-road straight shed. The new building was a 10-road straight shed. I recall the depot foreman's office was off-set between a very large brick wall and the only way in that we knew was via him. But, in those days, we had Melvin, and so with a buttery story Melvin, God bless him, got us in. Sadly,

In its original air-smoothed form, West Country class Pacific No. 34038 *Lynton* rests at 70A Nine Elms on Sunday, 2nd December, 1962. *(Alex Scott)*

Locomotives noted on Nine Elms shed, 70A, 1st July, 1962

Steam
57xx 0-6-0PT: 4601/72/81/5700
43xx 2-6-0: 6317
Hall 4-6-0: 4962/5912/90
M7 0-4-4T: 30032/5/51/2/241/5/9/320/1
T9 4-4-0: 30120
H16 4-6-2T: 30520
Lord Nelson 4-6-0: 30861/2
Schools 4-4-0: 30902/12/21/35/6/7
N class 2-6-0: 31408
U class 2-6-0: 31612/20/803
W class 2-6-4T: 31924
E4 0-6-2T: 32473/87/557
Q1 0-6-0: 33002/6/30/1
West Country 4-6-2: 34001/4/6/7/9/10/31/4/93/4/5
Battle of Britain 4-6-2: 34054/6/69/77
Merchant Navy 4-6-2: 35001/9/10/23/9
BR Class 5 4-6-0: 73086/9/110/1/4/6/8
BR Class 4 4-6-0: 75078
BR Class 4 2-6-4T: 80082

Diesel
Drewry 204hp 0-6-0 shunter: D2286
Warship Type 4: D812/54
BR 350hp 0-6-0 shunter: D3222/323/15217

Total Steam: 68 Diesel: 6

the depot closed in July, 1967.

My daughter and I soon found our way to another shed that my pals and I had bunked on Sunday 25th November, 1962. I took two photographs on Guildford shed which was a small semi-roundhouse. But it was not written down in my pad although the locomotives on Feltham were. The only explanation I have is whilst taking the photos in severe weather conditions, I forgot to note what was on the depot. At Feltham, however, I noted 30 steam locos and eight diesels. I copped 28.

Today nothing remains of the old six-road straight shed, the sidings lasted until late 1985 but the shed closed some time in July, 1967. The area has been landscaped in preparation for either a multi-storey shopping complex or a housing estate. I spoke to several people in the area and to be honest they all had different views on exactly what was going to be built. But one story interested me. Apparently some youngsters who were out playing in the shed vicinity came across and reported seeing several large lizards. Suddenly, the area became the focal point for scientists.

The old shed at 70C Guildford closed to steam on 9th July, 1967. Besides the semi-roundhouse it had a four-road through straight shed. The former steam shed area was redeveloped some time in 1988 and to this day it's commonly known for being The Fareham Road Car Park - how sad.

Once again, Ashleigh and I were on board another service, this time to Woking. On arrival, we were in luck because the Waterloo-Exeter service was running late and we were able to catch it.

Once on board, we found ourselves a nice quiet area and it was now time for some much-needed snap. The short journey to Basingstoke was very enjoyable. However, on arrival we soon set about seeing what was there now. The small three-road straight shed was bunked by M. & D. and myself on several occasions but I recall there was only ever a few on so we added them to the locomotives we had noted at Eastleigh. It was just a time-saving move but, on reflection, we should have put the numbers under the shed, which was coded 70D. It closed its doors to steam in March, 1963.

Today, the area has a totally different look, with a massive office block, a firm named Eurolink and another firm named Alland Fuel. In the yard some distance away from the old shed approach stands several rusting bogie bolster wagons. They have surely seen better days. It was time to bid Basingstoke a sad farewell and push on to Salisbury.

Ashleigh and I were beginning to feel rather tired by now but with four more depots to revisit we had to find that little bit extra to complete our trip. The heat only added to the tiredness and once we stepped off the train at Salisbury Ashleigh complained for the first time about how tired she really was.

There's no evidence today that the steam depot ever existed. Trees, bushes and undergrowth sway gently to and fro. Bumble bees and wasps busy themselves in and out of several colourful flowers on the site of the former Southern Region steam depot.

I only visited this depot on one occasion and that was with a railway society. We left from Station Street, close to New Street station, at midnight on Saturday 21st March, 1965. The trip by coach was called The South West Tour, and the coach was full. We arrived at Salisbury in the early hours of Sunday morning and were greeted by thick fog. We toured the depot and I noted 29 mixed steam and diesels on. I copped 12.

The party pushed on to several other sheds in the area but Ashleigh and I were now heading off in the direction of another depot I only visited the once, with the society. We soon arrived in the small town of Templecombe where the depot was coded 83G. On that Sunday way back in '65 I noted 15 on. We passed the depot, which was situated only a short distance from the

Locomotives on Templecombe shed, 83G, 21st March, 1965

Steam
2251 0-6-0: 3201
57xx 0-6-0PT: 4631/9670
Ivatt Class 2 2-6-2T: 41208/14/42/4
BR Class 4 4-6-0: 75008/72/3
BR Class 4 2-6-4T: 80039/43/59/67

Diesel
Western Type 4: D1032

Total Steam: 14 Diesel: 1

station. On arriving, I was very impressed with the station. Every available area was covered with beautiful flowers. "Pride in the job," I thought to myself.

I was just about to open the door for Ashleigh with one hand when my shed directory, which I was carrying in the other, nearly slipped from my grasp. I was fumbling with the door lock and as I fumbled a chap grabbed my directory as it was about to fall to the ground.

"Thankyou," I said.

"Blooming hell, I haven't seen one of those books for...," he enthused, then added: "It must be over forty-odd years. Off to the shed are you?," he enquired.

"Yes," I answered.

"I used to work on the old Southern Railway," he stated. "It's a Royal Navy installation of sorts," he advised me. "Yes, the firm who own it are called Plessey and they come under the Royal Naval authority." The advantage of this information I'd received from this ex-railway employee enabled us to stay on the train until we arrived at Yeovil.

This depot was situated on the left hand side of the down platform at Yeovil Junction station. The shed was coded 83E. On Sunday 21st March, 1965 I noted 12 mixed traction on the small three-road straight shed which closed in June, 1965.

Today, the South West Main Line company has built a brand new three-road building on the site of the former Southern Region depot. In the yard adjacent to the shed stood an old SR oil tank and, close by, an old guard's brake van. The building was locked so Ashleigh and I made our way over to the other station at Yeovil Pen Mill via two minibuses and a whole lot of flannel.

The last depot on our list was Weymouth, 70G. My first visit to this depot was on Sunday 21st March, 1965 when I was with the society. We bunked the shed on a very hot afternoon. I noted 25 mixed locos on and copped 12. I recall we bought a small plastic football from one of those ice cream parlours - cum - cafe - cum - shop. The lads and I played football on the beach before our return journey home to my beloved Birmingham.

The depot was chosen for a special duty apart from working the Weymouth-Waterloo services. It was destined to become a dumping ground for locomotives that were fast being discarded. It finally closed its doors to steam-hauled freight and passenger work on 9th July, 1967. Today, a housing estate sits on the site of the former steam shed. The station and surrounding area had totally changed since my last visit, which was about eight years ago.

I was once employed by BR at Weymouth, in the old warehouse that dealt with all the traffic for the Channel Islands. Today, there are new buildings sprouting up and they will soon join well established firms such as Comet, Halfords and B&Q, to mention just a few. Ashleigh and I spent three days in Weymouth, staying with my long-time friends Linda and Mike Rogan.

I recall sitting on Upwey and Broadway station as a young man, prior to the end of steam on the Southern Region. The double headed Standard named locomotives hauled the final steam expresses out of Weymouth to Waterloo until their final fling of that unforgettable steam era. I sat there with a couple of sandwiches, a bottle of pop, oh and an unopened packet of Jammie Dodgers, just for old time's sake. I never cried so much in all my life, apart from attending all my family and relatives' funerals.

The coach headed on towards another depot en-route to Birmingham on that super Sunday 21st March, 1965. We called in and bunked the little four-road, brick built straight shed at 83C Westbury. It had 20 locomotives on and I copped seven. It closed some time in September, 1965 so we were lucky in getting it in before closure. A small fuelling point was built on the site for diesel traction but that closed some years ago and today just a couple of permanent way machines sit there.

It's Wednesday morning 2nd August, 2000. Ashleigh and I are about to say a fond farewell to Linda and Mike. It's with a heavy heart that I say goodbye to them. We all shed a few tears prior to our departure. Eventually, the train pulled out of the station and we were homeward bound via a few more sheds. The house that I once lived in with my mom, dad and sister Sheila still stands. Sadly, my mom and dad no longer stand. They rest in peace together in a very beautiful spot down in Bognor Regis.

We arrived at our first port of call, Bournemouth, which was coded 70F when I, along with my fellow society members, arrived in the early hours of Sunday 21st March, 1965. The shed, situated only a brisk 10 minutes walk from Bournemouth Central station, was packed tight with 32 mixed engines on. I copped 17.

There was another station in the vicinity, Bournemouth West, but I never visited it. Sadly, the steam shed closed like many sister sheds around July, 1967. In fact the entire steam world started to disappear in the unforgettable month of July. Today it's a car park.

The stopping service we were now travelling on stopped at a very tidy station, Brockenhurst. I noticed an interesting coach standing in the dock. It looked like an old converted luggage van. There were several different sorts of cycles standing close by. A small sign stated that the bicycles were for hire for a small fee and one could cycle around the New Forest. Now I have no idea how large or small this forest is, but I didn't see many takers.

We arrived in Southampton just after dinner time. We had passed the Freightliner depot on our left and I noted several class 47s in the area, 47207, 47345 and 47287, plus two class 08s tucked away behind the 47s.

Once upon a time there were two main line stations in Southampton, Central and the Terminus. The latter ran non-stop boat trains to London Waterloo.

I only ever made one visit to the shed that was situated in Southampton Docks, coded 70L. The party was given special permission to visit the shed. I honestly believe we were just lucky that day. I wrote down 12 engine numbers but in all honesty I can't remember anything about the shed, except that I saw a couple of 0-4-0 shunters tucked inside a large cargo shed.

Today the area is part of the Ocean Park complex. There are a couple of maritime museums close by, but after asking several passers-by about the old three-road straight shed that closed in June, 1963, no-one had a clue what I was talking about. The closest I got to knowing the exact location of the site was from a chap whom I guess was in his sixties. He pointed to where he believed it to have been but it's anyone's guess if he was right.

The final shed Ashleigh and I were to visit on the south side of the river was at 75C Norwood Junction. I only visited this depot on one occasion and that was on Sunday 16th August, 1964. It was basically a freight depot and supplied engines for the once massive Norwood marshalling yard. Sadly, the five-road straight shed, which was situated close to Norwood station, closed to steam on 5th June, 1964. On my one and only visit I noted 17 mixed diesels on.

Today, there are several large buildings at the Selhurst end of the area. These depots service a variety of electric sets, I was told, for South West Trains, Silverlink, Connex South Central and a whole host of others.

If you stand on any platform at Clapham Junction you will observe so many different train companies with all their trains in different colours it'll make your head swim as they hurry and scurry through every few seconds. In its heyday, Clapham Junction handled 2,000 trains a day. On a sad note, the old overhanging signal box was removed some years ago. The only other one I can clearly remember was at Snow Hill, albeit that one was only small in comparison with Clapham's.

The firemen at Norwood Junction had menial duties to perform prior to the depot closing. They were officially moved to Nine Elms where they performed light engine movements and empty coaching stock turns. The last steam-hauled train from Norwood Junction was a freight train, but no-one I spoke to could recall its destination or the engine concerned. All rather sad.

Ashleigh and I boarded another fancy train to Willesden High Level. En-route we could clearly see the rear end of Old Oak Common shed as we headed off towards another great depot, 1A Willesden. I, along with M.&D. visited this depot on several occasions during the early Sixties, my earliest recording of the locomotives on shed being on Sunday 2nd December, 1962. I logged 26 diesel and 52 steam engines. I copped 12.

Today a single class 08 works the Freightliner depot that stands on the site of the old steam shed that sadly closed to steam on 27th September, 1965. The entire area was massive and consisted of a roundhouse and a 12-road straight shed, the old BR Staff Association Club still as close to the entrance as I can recall. The new depot, which is situated a short five-minute walk from the high level, only had a few locomotives visible as Ashleigh and I observed. They were 87016, 47783, 08890, 08918 and 47789.

On Sunday afternoon 1st July, 1962 M. & D. and I successfully bunked 81A Old Oak Common. We observed 85 mixed steam locomotives on plus 18 mixed diesels. I copped 29. Today, the area is still as massive as it was all those years ago but sadly, the steam engines are nowhere to be seen.

The depot had four enclosed roundhouses and a large carriage shed. A single turntable remains in full view but only a class 08 sits on one of the roads that once upon a time a King or a Castle rested. I managed to note several engine numbers before we left. They were 67018, 33232, 33113, 33202, 33021, 33205, 08865, 09016, 08389, 08825, 08541, 73107, 73128, 73141 and 73138. There were several other engines in the vicinity but we didn't want to push our luck. The shed closed to steam on 22nd March, 1965. A chap mentioned that a fellow named Harry Needle took over the workshops some years ago.

Locomotives noted on Old Oak Common shed, 81A, 1st July, 1962

Steam

County 4-6-0: 1010/2
15xx 0-6-0PT: 1503/4/6/7
Castle 4-6-0: 4077/82/5008/17/42/52/6/60/65/6/84/9/93/4/7000/9/13/26
47xx 2-8-0: 4704/8
Hall 4-6-0: 4948/89/91/5930/1/44/9/99/6959/73
King 4-6-0: 6009/10/1/16/21/5/7
61xx 2-6-2T: 6117/25/35/41/2/63/9
Grange 4-6-0: 6858/61
Modified Hall 4-6-0: 6998
94xx 0-6-0PT: 8420/59/86/9405/7/18/9/20/58/79
57xx 0-6-0PT: 3750/4/71/4615/8761/5/7/8/73/9659/61/9700/4/6/7/9/10/1
55/6/8/84

Diesel

English Electric Type 4: D340/81
BR Western Type 4: D1001/3
BR 350hp 0-6-0 shunter: D3030/2/3/114/599/601/2/947/4006/175
Beyer Peacock Type 3 Hymek: D7025/30/4
English Electric Type 1: D8010   ***Total*** Steam: 85   Diesel: 18

As Ashleigh and I were leaving the depot it started to rain very heavily so we increased our pace and quickly arrived at Willesden. The tube ride to Euston was very enjoyable until the on-board announcer stated that any passengers for Euston Square must change at Queens Road. We alighted there, only to be advised by the station staff to rejoin the train because the information on the tube was out of date. "Change at Baker Street," we were told, so we reboarded the tube train and set sail for Baker Street. Once we'd arrived safely at Baker Street and the doors flew open an announcement was made: "Attention, attention will all passengers please de-train."

We are slap bang in the middle of the teatime rush and there's hundreds of people all milling about trying to puzzle out why we're all standing on the platform. Another announcement advised us to re-train so everyone clambered back on board. The doors remained open which was very helpful to everyone on the train because, for the second time, we were told to de-train. Our train from Euston to Birmingham was looking a little doubtful by now.

Eventually, another announcement advised us the reason why everyone was standing about looking like a load of asylum seekers. Some kind hearted soul had left a package unattended at King's Cross. "How nice, how thoughtful, how f***ing stupid," I muttered to myself. Once on board, we hurried off towards Euston Square. Ashleigh and I had only minutes to spare and we ran like the wind up Euston Road to Euston station. On arrival we were lucky as they were just closing the last carriage door.

As the door closed tightly behind us, we were pulling out of the station. We walked the full length of the train before we found a seat in a smoking compartment. My luck was really out at this point and that's not the end of it. As our train sped on to Birmingham I had observed two lads acting very nervously, especially after we departed Watford. They were no doubt looking out for the ticket collector. The pair became very anxious when the guard approached as the train pulled into Coventry station.

"Tickets and all passes to be shown," I heard the guard call out.

The two lads cautiously made their way to the last door of the last carriage. No sooner had the train stopped, they were off like a shot. I observed them laughing as they passed by the window where we were sitting.

The journey from Coventry to Birmingham usually takes about 20 minutes so after all the excitement I could sit and relax a while, or so I thought. I couldn't believe my f***ing luck. Two scallywags have just bunked the train from London and bunked off at Coventry, now four really f***ing stupid b****s have just sat down to my left. These lads were surely aged in their early twenties and their behaviour had to be seen to be believed. In all honesty, if I'd had a gun I would have shot them just for a little peace and quiet.

After some serious words from the guard they did eventually pay for their tickets, albeit one of them made out he was deaf and dumb. The dumb part was correct. They even tried to fob the guard off with out-of-date passes but he held out and stood his ground against them. We finally arrived in New Street and it felt great to be home just like it did all those years ago when I, along with my two old school chums, arrived safely home from another daunting, daring, double death defying trip into the unknown - probably Wolverhampton.

Once indoors my wife asked us all about our trip to Weymouth. She knew from past experiences that our tale would be filled with one story after another.

Back home to New Street. Black Five 4-6-0 No. 45104 enters the station on 9th February, 1963. *(Alex Scott)*

I WASN'T ENTIRELY SATISFIED

My wife Carol is a field manager for a driving college and she has to visit a variety of areas around the country - London, Derby, Peterborough, Leeds and Newcastle. We were sitting down together eating our tea when out of the blue she surprisingly suggested that Ashleigh and I accompany her on a business trip to Gateshead. We would travel up on Monday 23rd October, 2000 and, after the meeting, we would stay overnight in an hotel. The next day we would travel back after she had finished her business in the area.

I must admit that since Ashleigh and I had arrived home from our visit to Newcastle in April, I had had a nagging feeling about not actually seeing Blyth staithes. Now an opportunity had arisen for us to go back and try to find the staithes for ourselves and finally put to rest the question as to whether or not they are really there.

We drove to Gateshead in the early hours of Monday 23rd October. On arriving there, my wife dropped us off and before she departed for her business meeting, we arranged to meet up at the Metro station around 5pm. Ashleigh and I purchased a ticket for the Metro and we spent the day sight-seeing, shopping and another trip down Memory Lane.

The rain decided to join us again as we walked from a very modern Tyne Dock station. I had my trusty shed directory in my hand and so off we toddled in search of the shed. It was only a few months ago that we covered this area but it's probably the last time I'll ever come here. As we approached a railway bridge close to the depot, I observed a chap standing on the bridge looking at the housing estate that now stands on the site of the former steam shed.

I knew exactly what he was doing. I know for a fact he was looking into the past. I know why he was doing it because I've done it myself and I can appreciate his most inner feelings. We approached him very slowly and once we stood by his side he was quick to notice us. I recall his grey hair being blown in different directions by a gust of wind. His face was very craggy and his steely eyes only gave way to a soft smile when he looked down on Ashleigh.

We never spoke. We just stood there side-by-side looking at the housing estate that the Nomad Housing Group had built. The estate was on the site of the old depot in Clive Street. The Housing Corporation has a sign erected near the railway bridge. The three of us just stood there looking deep into the past, a past that no doubt held something very special for this ageing gentleman.

Suddenly, he spoke: "Hello, what's your name?," he asked Ashleigh.

She smiled up at him and answered: "Ashleigh, and I'm thirteen years old."

A smile came to his face but behind his eyes I could see tears forming, tears of such sadness that I felt his pain and I felt a lump in my throat. I sniffled and momentarily I felt my eyes glass up.

That lingering smile down at Ashleigh invoked him to speak again: "My name's Alan, Mr. Alan Younger." He pointed towards the rows of houses then added: "My grandfather was an engine driver at the old steam shed. The shed comprised three brick built roundhouses and two other sheds. One was a five-road building, the other was attached to it and this was a four-road building. My grandfather used to take me round the shed where he'd show me the steam engines. Just over there stood Weddel Terrace. I remember the wash houses and the people who used them. I can still see folks coming and going," He concluded.

At that point he ruffled up Ashleigh's hair. Another smile came across his face before he turned away and walked several yards from where we had stood. I saw him stop close to the mesh fence that ran parallel to the housing estate and the main road. The next thing he did surprised me in an odd sort of way. He placed his ageing hands through the mesh fence and gripped it tightly. I felt sure he was trying so hard to reach out and perhaps touch the past, perhaps touch his grandfather.

Strangely, he reminded me of an internee. He stared intensely at the housing estate and I knew that somewhere lurking in his thoughts was an era that he was desperately trying to come to terms with. The last time I saw that sort of pain on a man's face was when I watched the film Ben Hur starring Charlton Heston. The man on the cross took the world's pain unto himself, and so did this man.

The rain was still falling as I took one final glance at the housing estate and Mr. Younger. We boarded the Metro and after several stops en-route we alighted at Gateshead. In its heyday the shed consisted of four-in-line brick-built roundhouses with a three-road dead ended shed. In 1956 the roundhouses were converted to a smaller two-roundhouse building, and rebuilt again on dieselisation to a nine-road shed.

The shopping centre was very busy and I noticed the time on a clock in a jewellers shop. It was almost 4.15pm. The day had whizzed by and now Ashleigh wanted to try on a coat that she had noticed in a small clothes shop. The coat was named Peter Storm, and according to Ashleigh they were all the rage at her school back in Brum. The cost was £40.

"Forty quid, forty quid," I mumbled to myself. "What could I have done with forty quid 30 years ago?" She's still wearing the coat to school today.

After a very expensive shopping spree we met up with my wife at Gateshead Metro. The short drive to her hotel was a pleasurable one because we exchanged data on our day. The hotel was dead smart, so was the meal which my wife paid for on her firm's account. Nice one.

After a good night's sleep and a very enjoyable breakfast, my wife went off to work. Ashleigh and I had arranged to meet up with her later in the day and try to get to Blyth.

The time was approaching 8.48am when my wife dropped us off at Heworth station. We boarded the Middlesbrough-bound service that travelled via Sunderland. The fare for the both of us came to £7.30. I never saw a single freight train between Heworth, Middlesbrough, Darlington, Newcastle and Heworth. There was a handful of diesels on Thornaby shed and a single class 66 at Tyne Yard.

In the days of steam all manner of rolling stock would have passed us. The amount of mineral trains arriving and departing a thousand and one sidings must have totalled thousands. The staff that once worked on the railways nationwide surely totalled millions. In those days, a job on the railway was a job for life and a regular pay packet. Those who worked on the railways worked with so much pride and passion it spoke volumes for their forefathers who built this country on railways.

My charming wife arrived spot on time at Heworth Metro. Ashleigh and I joined her and we sped northwards until we arrived in the quaint little village of Blyth. I spoke to several people in the area and they all agreed that the staithes were still there. I must have spoken to about 20 people on the subject. By now I was absolutely sure that they were still intact.

We drove from the north side of Blyth to the south side. I kept a sharp lookout as we ventured closer and closer to the staithes. We stopped about a quarter of a mile from where they should have stood. Blyth power station stood on our right hand side. Carol stopped the car whilst I made my final enquiry about the staithes. The two security guards working in their office agreed that the staithes were still standing.

The power station was only a quarter of a mile from where the staithes were supposedly standing. "A quarter of a mile away, a quarter of a mile away," I mumbled to myself.

"It's only a quarter of a mile away," I informed my wife as I slipped into our car. I was overcome with excitement as we drove towards the staithes.

Locomotives noted on North and South Blyth sheds, 52F, 24th February, 1963

Steam

Q6 0-8-0: 63352/6/9/81/6/429
J27 0-6-0: 65792/4/801/8/10/9/20/2/8/34/
        65855/7/61/75/9/80/9/90/1/3

Diesel

BR 204hp 0-6-0 shunter: D2090/105/66

Total   Steam: 26   Diesel: 3

Class J27 0-6-0 No. 65808 peeps out of the straight shed at South Blyth on Sunday 24th February, 1963. *(Alex Scott)*

On arrival, I couldn't believe my eyes. "F***k it!," I said as tears started to fall. "They're gone."

I felt my heart slump to its lowest ever point and the blood drain from my veins. For a split second I felt my heart stop. I couldn't believe that they had gone after everyone I'd spoken to said they were still intact.

My wife spoke, saying: "Alex, I wanted to see them."

Ashleigh tried to comfort me when she added: "Dad, I honestly wanted to see them after you'd explained in detail what they looked like."

I would have liked to have met Mr. George Tuffs. I was told about him, apparently the local expert on the staithes and one of the last teamers to work there. Teamers were unique among railwaymen. Responsible for ensuring that coal was evenly loaded into the ships' holds, they had their own pay and conditions, and could earn good money, being paid by the ton loaded. Their skill went back long before the dawn of main line railways.

Coal has been shipped from Blyth for over 600 years. The first known elevated point for loading boats was constructed in 1788. The first timber staithes were built by the Tyne & Blyth Junction Railway on the south side of the river in 1849. With this, coal shipping through Blyth became a big industry, reaching 200,000 tons a year. The North Eastern Railway added more staithes in 1888 and by 1898 Blyth was shipping over 3 million tons from an increasing number of Northumberland pits. Another set of staithes at North Blyth, the West staithes, were completed in 1928 by the LNER while the Cowpen Coal Company opened a deep water berth at South Blyth in the 1930s. Coal shipments continued to increase and, surprisingly, Blyth did not reach its peak until 1961 when, as Europe's biggest coal port, it shipped 6.9 million tons. Yet closures began just three years later and by 1968 there had been a big decline in the amount of coal shipped. North and South Blyth sheds closed on 27th January, 1968, followed the next day by the opening of the new Cambois diesel depot. Further closures took place in the 1970s until only the West Blyth staithes remained in operation. BR extensively modernised two berths in 1983 by which time most of the coal was being shipped to power stations in the London area. But this did not stem the decline and BR made the last shipment of coal from the staithes at North Blyth on 31st December, 1989.

The tradition did not end, however. The reason for the staithes' closure was that British Coal's Opencast Executive, their main user, had decided to concentrate shipments on their own brand new deep water berth at South Blyth for which they also bought the South Blyth branch line from BR.

Mr. George Tuffs and the West Blyth staithes at the time of their closure in 1989. *(Stephen Chapman)*

I NEVER COVERED ALL EIGHTEEN BUT I DID COVER THIRTEEN

I recall there used to be eighteen steam sheds in the capital but Melvin, David and I only bunked 13, and I can only prove that I bunked nine. However, my word has always been good and I have no reason to lie. In my four remaining pads I can prove that we bunked those nine. The days and dates will go some way in clarifying the truth, plus the locomotives recorded for posterity and the photos I took at a variety of depots whilst there.

The usual routine was for the three of us to meet up at the old ticket office at Snow Hill station on a Sunday morning around 9.45am. We usually whizzed round the station collecting any locos that were awaiting departure prior to our train being announced. The lady announcer would announce our train at exactly 9.54: "The next train to arrive on platform number seven will be for London Paddington." We turned our eyes towards the Wolverhampton direction.

Suddenly, there it was, the purest of pure white smoke spiralling skywards, the sound of the whistle announcing its approach. The sunbeams bouncing off its bright green paintwork. The warmth of its boiler and the heat from its firebox on a beautiful summer's morning added to this sight of sights. It was an unforgettable sound as it came closer and closer. Then, there it was, a gleaming King class locomotive resting next to platform seven, a rake of chocolate and cream coaches encouraging one and all to board.

The Kings worked some crack express trains in those halcyon days. The Cambrian Coast Express, the Red Dragon and no doubt many, many others. But whatever happened to those beautiful and much loved locomotives of yesteryear? The three survivors are 6000 *King George V*, 6023 *King Edward 11* and 6024 *King Edward 1*. The remaining locomotives were cut up at the following scrapyards:

The firm of Cox & Danks at Langley Green, Oldbury, Warley in Worcestershire cut up Nos. 6001, 6002, 6007, 6012, 6014, 6015, 6016, 6017, 6020, 6022 and last but not least, 6027. Swindon works very reluctantly cut up 6003, 6004, 6006, 6008, 6010, 6011, 6013, 6018, 6025 and 6026. Cashmore's at Newport, Monmouthshire cut up 6009, 6019, 6021 and 6029, and No. 6005 was cut up at Cashmore's yard at Great Bridge, Tipton, Staffs. Finally, Birds of Risca, Newport, cut up 6028. Oh so sad.

We were usually the first people to scurry into a welcoming compartment. Once inside we opened our rucksacks, then we'd get out some of our snap, followed by our pads, pens and my unopened packet of Jammie Dodgers which didn't stay unopened for long. David and Melvin enjoyed them tremendously, and I managed to tuck into the odd one now and then.

Today, it's Sunday 5th November, 2000. It's a very crisp morning, typical of the time of year. I can't remember the last time my wife and three daughters travelled together in our car on a journey with me. We departed our front door at 8am. After scoffing most of their snap en-route, they slept most of the way until we arrived and parked close to the Motorail terminal at London Paddington. The time was 9.45am, the parking fee £9. A bleeding cheek if you ask me!

We all agreed to meet up at the electric departure boards at 4.30pm. My family were going to spend the day at the Dome. I was going to finish off my last adventure around several sheds that Melvin, David and I visited in the early Sixties. The depots I intended to revisit were 30A Stratford, 34G Finsbury Park, 34A King's Cross, 14D Neasden, 14A Cricklewood and 14B Kentish Town. I started by purchasing a £4.70 One Day Travel Card, then bade farewell to my wife and children and headed off to Stratford.

The overall picture across the country was one of total chaos. Floods had been with us for several weeks. There was chaos on the railways following the train crash at Hatfield and the resulting nationwide speed restrictions and engineering works. A fuel crisis was imminent but the severe winter of 1962/63 never stopped us train spotting, so a mere handful of problems wasn't going to stop me.

I arrived at Stratford and quickly made my way to the gaffer's office. On arrival I introduced myself to several locomen who were talking inside the booking-on point. I produced my book Fearless Ghosts as proof of identity.

I was taken aback by the interest shown by two drivers who made it known to me that they had purchased the book and they recognized the cover immediately. It was handshakes all round.

I explained my reasons for visiting the depot and after gaining permission to enter legally, I was escorted round by Mr. Les Bond. Les had been at the depot since moving there from Cambridge in the early Sixties, so I was in great company.

"Alex, there were several buildings on this vast site in steam days. It was the largest grouping of buildings in Europe. At one point there were 300 locomotives allocated here," Les advised me passionately.

I glanced around the forlorn looking area that surely held a million and one railway stories. The steam sheds that held us kids spellbound were long gone. The maintenance depot that housed only a class 31 and an 08 shunter looked and felt so eerie. A coldness came over me as we strolled around this once busy part of the depot.

A line of derelict diesels stood awaiting their fate outside in the yard. Class 31s, 37s, 47s and 08s. Modern traction, in the guise of class 56s and 66s stood awaiting their next turn of duty. Les pointed to a building that he

The Polygon building at Stratford depot on 5th November, 2000.
Back in 1950, 383 locomotives were based at Stratford, 30A, probably the biggest allocation in the world. The shed closed to steam in September, 1962 but I found a few steam locos there, probably stored, during my only visit on 24th March, 1963. *(Alex Scott)*

affectionately called "The Polygon Building." I gazed upwards at this oddly designed building. I'm sure Les knew I was puzzled to say the least.

"Alex, come with me and take a closer look," he beckoned.

I followed him as we entered one room, then another and another until we had inspected every room except one. "Alex, this is the old gaffer's room. That's the booking-on point. The store room was there, the trainmen's room over there, tool room just there and the fitters' room was there."

The final room he pointed out was by far the most interesting. The story Les was about to tell held my interest throughout.

"Alex, the room was purpose built for one reason, and one reason only, to sleep in," he stated with a wry smile on his face. I smiled at the very thought of a load of railwaymen all kipping down in this room. Les continued between my smiling and tongue-in-cheek looks: "Yes, they only slept in that room because they'd either finished their turn of duty in the early hours of the morning and there was no night service home, or their booked turn of duty was in the early hours of the morning and they had no transport to get them to work in time, so they came in early, got their heads down until it was time to book on," he concluded.

There was an archway underneath the building and I felt sure it had some relevance to the design so I asked Les about it. "Les, the archway, what's the story behind it?"

We walked back through the archway and after walking through it, he answered me: "It's just a short cut."

At that point we both burst out laughing. "Come on Alex, I'll show you around the rest of the depot." I followed him, still tittering.

I continued following him to where the main entrance to the double-ended maintenance building stood idle.

"Stop right there," Les announced seriously and sternly.

I stopped on a sixpence.

"Now then," Les added. "Where you are standing is the actual spot where the Channel Tunnel Rail Link will come up." He stretched out his right arm and turned full circle. "Alex, by April, 2001 all you see before you will be gone." The word 'gone' had sadness attached to it. I observed his eyes glass up momentarily as we headed towards the old workshops.

"The works closed down around the end of 1990. A timber firm now occupies this massive building where they had the most up to date machinery for lifting the heavy steam locomotives from their wheels. When steam faded into the annals of history so the machinery lifted the diesel and electric locomotives upwards so they could be repaired. Heavy duty and light engineering duties were once performed here," Les concluded sadly.

A lengthy pause fell between us because I knew that the story of this one-time fantastic shed was hurting him to tell me. "The firm of Balfour Beatty have the contract to redevelop the entire area. The two Victorian gasometers that overlook King's Cross and St. Pancras stations are being dismantled to make way for the Channel Tunnel project commencing from St. Pancras and running via Stratford to Lee Bridge."

We covered the rest of the depot and we came across five of the largest fuel containers that I personally ever saw. A massive snowplough stood rusting quietly in a maze of overgrowth. Les quipped: "Not much need for them these days." A wry smile came across his face and another short pause before he told me about the new depot: "A new depot is being built on the site of the old marshalling yard at Temple Mills."

At that point, we entered the gaffer's office where he showed me the schematic for the entire area covering Stratford and the new depot. I felt really privileged to be looking over the future of this depot and a deep sense of pleasure because it did have a future.

I shook hands with everyone in the office and I was choked up when the gaffer invited me back at any time. I felt embarrassed at how everyone had gone out of their way to help me in my summing up of the largest depot in Europe. The word Europe will live on in the future of this awesome depot.

I thanked Les and we parted with a friendly handshake. "Oh, one last heyday it employed almost five thousand people. There were over three hundred locomotives allocated here. They even had a chemical room where they developed cleaning materials." He paused, then said: "Goodbye Alex, see you mate."

In steam days Melvin, David and I only bunked this shed once and that was on Sunday 24th March, 1963. Diesel locomotives were very much in evidence as we made our way around the shed but we did record a handful of steam locos still in steam and awaiting their next turns of duty. A total of 110 mixed traction were recorded that day and I copped 96. I have only one regret, I would have loved to have seen this depot in its heyday.

Today, I've just arrived at Finsbury Park. I have my trusty shed directory in hand, so off I go. On arrival, I observe that a new housing estate has sprung up on the site of the former diesel depot. But on Sunday 24th March, 1963 we noted 23 mixed diesels on shed.

The next depot I visited was King's Cross Top Shed. Today, the Castle Cement terminal sits on the former engine shed that the three of us bunked several times but, because I mislaid my old school books, the numbers were lost forever. My first pad contains 53 steam engines and 17 diesels that were on on Sunday 1st July, 1962. I copped 41.

The next three depots we bunked in those great days of steam were once again in the early Sixties. The depot at Cricklewood consisted of two enclosed roundhouses and closed to steam on 19th December, 1964. Kentish Town shed was a roundhouse and closed its doors to steam in April, 1963. Finally, Neasden was a six-road straight shed and closed on either 18th or 19th June, 1963.

Once again, I have no proof of our visit but I recall we did visit and bunk these three sheds. Today, Parcel Force and Union Railways are situated close to Cricklewood depot, so I have been informed. Murphy's, the building firm now occupy the old roundhouse that was once Kentish Town. Neasden bus depot stands on the site of the old steam shed.

By now, my spirits were at an all-time low. The weather had been very kind to me and as I headed towards Paddington and my waiting family my thoughts were on today and yesteryear. Visions of steam depots bunked and of Melvin and David racing and chasing around depots nationwide brought a wry smile to my face. I was no longer a little lad scurrying in and out of depots with all the confidence in the world, a world of steam engines, diesels and happy times.

Today, my confidence is just as it was some 40-odd years ago. My enthusiasm has never dwindled as far as this greatest of hobbies is concerned. But now I'm older and in some respects wiser. I'd give my life for just one step back into the past and just to observe it all again just one more time before I go. Oh, what a request.

THE CHICKEN RUN

It was a Saturday and Carol and Ashleigh and I were travelling home from Nottingham to Birmingham after a Christmas shopping spree. As we approached our turnoff to join the motorway I noticed, in the distance, Toton depot and suggested that we take a look.

I never did this depot in steam days but remember passing it on a diverted train in the 1960s.

On arrival, we were confronted by a security officer inside a cabin. I spoke to him and he advised me that unless I had a permit there was no way I was going any further than his office.

Just then an engineman going off duty popped into the office to speak to the security guard on a private matter. As he was about to leave, I approached him and explained that I was the author of the recently published book Fearless Ghosts.

He responded by saying jovially: "I suppose you want all the loco numbers mate?"

I smiled and said yes.

"Hang on," he said.

At that point he drove me towards the depot and returned with a list of locos in and around the depot area. I thanked him, shook his hand and bade him farewell. It was at that point that he turned round and told me about a group of lads playing "chicken" across the main lines that run past the depot. One of them, I believe he was only 11, slipped in front of an oncoming train. This proved fatal for the chicken runner. He died just before Christmas, 1999.

Trains are not toys. They can, and they will kill you or maime you for the rest of your life so please, please don't trespass on the railway - it is not a playground or a public thoroughfare. In our day, Melvin, David and I were lucky. This young lad wasn't.

The shed in question on page 22 was 17B Burton. the depot consisted of two enclosed roundhouses. It closed to steam in 1966